Survival Wellness Advocacy and the BIG WIN

A Supplemental Guide for Surviving the Planet X Tribulation

D0830619

Survival Wellness Advocacy and the BIG WIN

A Supplemental Guide for Surviving the Planet X Tribulation

Your Own World Books
Nevada USA

PlanetXTribulation.com
YowBooks.com

Copyright

Survival Wellness Advocacy and the BIG WIN: A Supplemental Guide for Surviving the Planet X Tribulation

First Edition – January 2017
Marshall Masters

Your Own World Books
An imprint of Knowledge Mountain Church
of Perpetual Genesis, NV, USA
planetxtribulation.com
yowbooks.com

Trade Paperback
ISBN-13: 978-1542447966
ISBN-10: 1542447968

Notices

Trademarks

Table of Contents

Marshall's Motto

Destiny comes to those who listen,
and fate finds the rest.

So learn what you can learn,
do what you can do,
and never give up hope!

1

You and Me

As you read these words, I know one thing about you for certain. You are either an imposter seeking self-advantage or a wonderful person of great sensitivity and insight. As for the imposters, they will quickly lose interest; so, I shall not speak to them. Rather, I shall speak to you as a sensitive person in awareness because you will serve a very precious and special role in the coming tribulation.

Being in service to your role is my mission for writing this book. I want to empower you so that you can become a decisive force for positive change. This is because you have it within you to become a valued member of a survival community in a role comparable to those of Native American medicine men and women if you so choose. And if you decide to limit your focus to the needs of your loved ones, this book offers you several helpful and unique insights to achieve those aims.

Nonetheless, my focus will be on those of you who are sensitives in awareness and interested in being in service to spiritual survival communities and for the betterment of humankind. As such, you will understand the power that one finds in the subtleties of life, and you will be valued and respected for that. This is because during the difficult years to come, the possession of things will be less important than the knowing of things. As the old axiom goes, "Knowledge is power." Yet, when all that one can find in a pant pocket is lint, it's hard to imagine the wisdom of this enduring axiom.

Therefore, let me tell you the first thing that I know about you as a sensitive. In most every case you possess a big heart and a small wallet, and the pressing material needs for bullets, beans, and bunkers often overwhelms you with a sense of despair.

If so, my mission in writing this book for you as someone who is sensitive and in awareness is to fill your heart with hope for the future and a simple message: if you cannot afford a hill of beans, then you shall learn how to become worth your weight in beans. When you have finished reading this book, you will understand that this is a true path and not wishful thinking.

The second thing that I know about you as a sensitive in awareness is that you will likely feel isolated and distanced from like-minded others. If so take heart; for you are but one of a growing and vibrant minority of precious individuals. Since 1999 I have spoken with countless numbers of you and have come to know the truth of the matter. So, what is that truth?

While you may believe that you are isolated, what I see is a chorus of hope for the future that is spread all across the globe because each of you can play a vital role in God's plan. The reason why you are so distant from your brothers and sisters in awareness is because in divine wisdom, God keeps you safe from those of evil intent who would see this divine plan fail.

The third thing I know about you is that the vast majority of you in awareness have been so for several years and that many of you have been in awareness since you were young children. You are likely to be between the ages of 45 to 65.

The fourth thing I know about you is that many of you are grandparents with grown children and grandchildren living in areas of certain doom. If this is you, I know that your heart is torn because your progeny will inevitably and arrogantly refuses to heed your concerns.

If this is you, it is a living agony because you feel that you cannot afford to do for them what they must do for themselves and that they will perish. A fate that leaves you only two choices: to die with them in a futile gesture of love, or to live with an ache in your heart that will eventually sap your will to live. If so, take heart, for when you have finished reading this book, you will understand that there is a way to save them and that this is a true path and not wishful thinking.

Therefore, as a sensitive in awareness, I already know a great many things about you. I've spoken with many of you over the years, and you have frankly shared your joys and agonies with me; in turn I've always listened and always cared. While each conversation is unique, each is the same in one respect. I never end the conversation without hearing in your voice that you now know you are not alone.

So, as we move forward together, you will know what I already know about you. But what I do not know about you is your stage of awareness. As with many things, awareness is a developmental process through several phases. Likewise, each journey is unique. An old axiom tells us, "To the heart of a great mystery, many roads lead."

So, we understand that you are following your road to this great mystery and I'm following mine. The question now becomes where are we relative to each other and the heart of this great mystery? This is not as some would assume to establish a rank but responsibility. Because those who have traveled further along their paths and have come closer to this great mystery have the responsibility of sharing what they have learned with those more distant.

This is the point of what I'm doing with this book. It is to share with those of you more distant what I have learned on my journey that began in the 1990's. Gauging this distance is easier than you might first imagine.

The Five Stages of Catastrophism

Those of us who are in awareness have a compass of the soul so to speak that helps us determine our proximity to the great mystery we seek. I first discussed this in my documentary titled, *Precognition and the Five Stages of Catastrophism* (2010). Those five stages are:

- Stage 1: I do not have time for this crap.
- Stage 2: Oh, crap!
- Stage 3: Share the crap
- Stage 4: Crap happens
- Stage 5: The universe is unfolding as it should.

After releasing the video in August 2010, I wondered if I had overused the word "crap." When I asked many of those who watch the video and enjoyed it, if I should find a more eloquent word, they all told me that it was exactly the right word and that I should use it.

The reaction was mixed. Those in denial panned it because it offended their self-imposed life bubble's sensibilities, whereas those well along in their paths of awareness always tell me that it is the best thing I've done. I invite you to watch it and see for yourself, but in the meantime let's use this five stage work to briefly illustrate my journey.

Stage 1 – I Do Not Have Time for This Crap

I first realized my awareness during the election of 1960. A precocious 2nd grader I remember the day. As my older sister dressed me for school, she tells me how she was supporting John F. Kennedy even though she was not then old enough to vote. "We need to help Kennedy win," she said emphatically.

Without even giving it a moment's thought I answered, "No, he must not win."

My sister was shocked, "What on earth makes you say that?" she demanded.

Again, without giving it a moment's thought, I replied, "Because if he wins, he will be killed." I knew it at that moment. With as much certainty as one would know his or her name and as history shows us, what I experienced was a profound moment of precognition.

For this reason I was never one to mock or ridiculed those who were in awareness, as I often saw happen with others. On the other hand I was so wrapped up in trying to be a successful consumer automaton that I just didn't pay attention. That would all change in the 1990's.

Stage 2 – Oh Crap!

Stage two of awareness is essentially a perceptive event, or a series of perceptive events leading to an epiphany that forever changes your worldview. For those of you in awareness this process is about as pleasant as being slapped across the face with the dead salmon. It is not something you necessarily wish to declare as your college major.

This process of awakening is something that you come to realize is the result of a decision you made before you were born (and this will be discussed in greater detail later in the book). But for now let's just make clearly one point:

This process leads you down a predictable path towards a completely unpredictable result. This is your epiphany of awareness.

For me that process began in the early 90's when I started a travel business to Russia after the downfall of the Soviet Union. Over the course of several years I would fly from San Francisco to Moscow on Aeroflot, via the polar around. The trip over in December was always at night, and the trip back in January was always during the day; so I remember that first return trip.

I grew up in the desert of Phoenix, Arizona and all that I knew about snow was you had to drive somewhere to find it. But this was the first time, when looking through the window of an Ilyushin Il-62 airliner, that I saw blue glacial ice; I was mesmerized. After all when I was a kid, blue ice was something that you bought in a snow cone with colored syrup at the local convenience store.

That first trip was incredible because from horizon-to-horizon it was a pristine and perfect polar world. That was in 1993. I flew the same route at the same time of year every year until 1999 when I beheld what can only be called a tragic scene. What had once been perfect and pristine had over the years and in a consistent manner degraded until in that final trip, the North Pole look like the broken windshield of a car in a wrecking yard.

This was my "Oh crap!" moment. The blinders were now off. I decided then that I was not going to believe the major corporations propaganda; I would understand what I had seen with my own eyes over the previous several years – that our world is changing in a very disturbing way. The question then became what would I do about it? Again, the universe led me down a predictable path to an unpredictable result.

Stage 3 – Share the Crap

It was my fortune to be the first one in the neighborhood to have high-speed DSL Internet, and being a geek at heart, I decided to test it using websites about the prophecies of Nostradamus. I did not know that much about his prophecies, and frankly, I was not that interested. All I knew was that these early websites had a lot of graphics and were poorly designed. This meant they would be as slow as sludge on a dial-up modem. On the other hand they should snap to attention with DSL speed. So, I began reading and this led me to the King of Terror prophecy.

It was a prediction of Nostradamus that during a solar eclipse in the year of the prophecy the King of Terror comet would reveal itself. Using a NASA video feed of the eclise as seen from Turkey, I discovered the comet behind the sun, during that eclipse. Over a decade later, I would once again find evidence of Planet X, lurking behind the sun as well.

My 1999 King of Terror findings were published by an independent alternative science site called The Millennium Group and received over 5 million hits. That success proved to be my share the crap moment, when I first began writing on alternative science topics, which led to the creation of my site, Your Own World USA in December 1999. Since then, I've never looked back.

This is not to say it is a pleasant experience because stage three is the worst of the three stages. This is because people sound the alarm and try to explain what they have learned to people who are still in stage one. If this is you, then you have been mocked, and ridiculed. You now feel isolated despite all of the threats of punishment if you persist.

This is also a time when those who have a spouse in denial will often hear the nuclear threat. "Stop this, or I'll divorce you." Those in awareness will just lower their heads and soldier on, doing this in the hope that things will change – but they never do. That is until crap happens.

Stage 4 – Crap Happens

You know you are in stage IV when you realize that sharing the crap is a one-way ticket to isolation and misery. So you just resolve yourself to accept your fate in silence and isolation. This is when many in awareness with a spouse in denial who is badgering them with the nuclear threat of divorce, actually become the first ones to file the papers.

For me, stage four began after I published my article Did Planet X / Nibiru Kill the Dinosaurs in January 2002. It was my first article on Planet X, and Dr. Brian Marsden, Associate Director of the Smithsonian Astrophysics Observatories, helped me with the research.

After that, I was no longer an environmental tree hugger with a genuine concern for earth changes. I had moved straight out to the fringe as a Planet X researcher, author, and publisher. That was when I resigned myself to a largely thankless study of Planet X and the tribulations it has caused for our planet.

When you're in stage four, you are resigned to your fate. What you study is joyless, and certainly not inspiring, yet you are compelled to move forward. Not in the manner that one would be visually captured by an unfolding train wreck, but rather because you come to understand that this path of knowledge is important and deserving of sacrifice. This is the way it was for me until 2008.

Stage 5 – The Universe Is Unfolding As It Should

The difficulty with being in stage IV is what prolongs it. It is a persistent compulsion to follow the science alone, and this limited focus will only lead you to one conclusion, despair. Why was this the case for me? The science was telling me that all of the Planet X suppression, propaganda, misinformation, and manipulation by powerful elites had only one purpose. It was to ensure the maximum number of people perish during the tribulation.

Living with this epiphany was the most difficult and hopeless time in my life. It seemed to me that they would inevitably be successful. However, I could not give up for the very reason that many endured the dark days of World War II. The old adage is, "winners never quit and quitters never win." I just could not quit. Rather, I soldiered on clinging to the hope that one day I would find an answer that would take me beyond despair.

That finally happened in 2008, after I published my book, *Planet X Forecast and 2012 Survival Guide*. I had read an interesting article about how several Nobel laureates began searching through paranormal studies for the answers that science could not provide. As a self-described born hard geek, that article waved a green flag for me, and the race was on.

I, and a few others who shared my interest, begin doing paranormal research with gifted psychics who could channel entities. We developed a protocol for the study and a precise and measurable way to vet the ethereal entities. It is important to note that in each and every case, we were able to vet the entities without exception.

One such entity was an ancient Egyptian temple priest by the name of Serapis Bey. What propelled this personal study was my sense of hopelessness that still tormented me. Billions of people would die because they were engineered to that fate. What I was hoping for was a game changer to alter that outcome and Serapis Bey delivered.

What he told me with the assistance of a gifted and noble channeler, was the following:

> "Marshall, the book of humankind is a vast book of many, many chapters, and it is far from being complete. As with all books, this edition has many chapters and the present chapter belongs to the elites and there is nothing you can do about that. It is theirs and can never be taken from them; do not waste your energy attempting to do so. Rather, what you need to understand is that all chapters like all books come to an end and that this present chapter is close to its end. The elites know that, and they also know that the next chapter does not belong to them. It is yours by destiny, but only if you seize it. The elites know this as well, and if they are to perpetuate their dominance over your species, they must find a way to bluff you into giving away your future. They will be clever, but if humankind calls their bluff, they are certain to lose. Let this be where you invest your time and energy."

In closing the session, I asked Serapis Bey a predefined vetting question. "Give me a significant weather event that is at least six months out from today?"

Serapis Bey predicted that in six months a typhoon in the Pacific would head towards the Baja California Peninsula. It would then suddenly veer off course and head straight for San Diego. It would then either dissipate at sea or reach land as a strong wind storm. Six months later the typhoon appeared as predicted, veered towards San Diego, and then dissipated at sea.

Once I had vetted Serapis Bey, there was no further doubt in my mind that we have a way to bridge from the despair of science to the hope of spirit; this was the day that I entered stage five with the solemn and joyous epiphany that the universe truly is unfolding as it should.

Since then, I slowly began transitioning from pure science reporting to a mix of science and spirituality. Both are necessary to the task at hand for those who survive the tribulation. That task is the unshackling our species which has been enslaved for countless generations so that we can have a post tribulation world of enlightenment, that Star Trek future that so many of us hope for.

But what if humanity fails to call the bluff and the elites bridge between the chapters they own to one to which they were never entitled? Humanity will then suffer through the tribulation in a missed moment of freedom only to be shackled into slavery once again for countless generations. This will last until such a time as our planet has been laid waste and is of no value. Only then will some future generation be left to enjoy their freedom in a dying world.

Free Will

Since having that epiphany so many years ago, all that I do and hope for is for those precious few who survive the tribulation will call the bluff, and they will say "no" to the elites' inducements. That will only lead us back into slavery. They must understand that they are not saying "no" to the carrot, but rather, "no" to the stick.

So this is where I am at this moment on my path towards that great mystery we all seek. That being said; now is your moment to take your compass heading. How far along are you in awareness? What stage have you reached? But even more importantly, what are you prepared to do?

If all that you are prepared to do is to take care of only you and yours, then I hope you will find value in this book. Because, despite what you think, the *me-and-mine* prepper path is more certain to lead you to doom than you could ever imagine. This is because me-and-mine preppers fail to understand that they will be easy targets for the predator groups during the early years of the tribulation. But then, this is your right because what is more precious than life itself, *free will*.

That being said, it is my free will choice to focus all of my attention, moving forward, upon those in awareness who feel drawn to a noble purpose. Do not yet despair that you lack the financial wherewithal for me-and-mine prepping. This book will open your mind to new and priceless possibilities. Why do I share this with you? Because, all that I have learned and all that I believe in my heart tells me that you are one of God's many messengers of hope and for this, I dearly love you so.

Marshall Masters
Chief Steward
Knowledge Mountain
Church of Perpetual Genesis

Part 1 –
Destiny and
Freedom

Your Destiny as an Advocate

In the previous chapter I told you that "you are one of God's many messengers of hope." Did that pique your curiosity? Let's proceed on the assumption that it did, and that you are curious and asking yourself "what is the meaning of this." To answer this question, let's begin with your life for this is where the answer is to be found.

Was there a time when you had foreknowledge of a future event in other words, precognition? Or was it a dream, or vision, or premonition that gave you a strong feeling that something unpleasant was about to happen? If so, were you hesitant in admitting that to yourself let alone sharing it with others?

A soothsayer is a person that is supposed to foresee the future. For the better part of human history those with this gift held cherished positions of respect within their communities and clans. Not because they were always accurate, but because on balance, they were accurate enough to make a positive difference in the outcomes. As a sensitive in awareness, you possess this ability even though it may not have awakened in you. This ability has nonetheless steered you onto your destiny path whether you wish to admit it or not. As a way to illustrate this, I will share my personal story.

Wall of Water

I am a survivor of the 1989 World Series earthquake which is also known as the Loma Prieta earthquake which struck the San Francisco Bay Area. It happened during the opening to the third game at Candlestick Park. At the time I was a few miles south of the ballpark when the quake claimed 63 lives and injured 3,757 others. Fortunately for me, I was not physically injured, but I did spend the next six months looking up at the ceiling as I lay in bed, wondering what it would feel like to wear it.

In retrospect the most remarkable aspect of that experience actually occurred two weeks earlier, when I experienced a profound precognitive experience. At the time I lived in an apartment in the southwest corner of San Francisco a few blocks from the beach. Returning home from work, I turned off Highway 280 onto John Daly Blvd, and as I was crossing the overpass, I saw a wall of water approaching the western shores of San Francisco from as far as I could see in both directions.

It was so real and so frightening that at that moment I actually thought I was seeing my impending death. Shaken, I immediately pulled into the emergency lane and stopped as the vision persisted for several more seconds. Then it vanished; once again all I saw was the clear blue sky and the western edge of the city before me.

That memory stayed with me, and to this day I can still see it in my mind. So in February 2004 when I decided to start my Cut to the Chase podcast, my first interview was with Jim Berkland, a USGS Geologist, who had accurately predicted the earthquake within an hour of when it actually occurred. The topic of the interview was the activity at Yellowstone; it was also the very first time I publicly used the motto I coined which I dubbed Marshall's Motto:

Destiny comes to those who listen, and fate finds the rest.

So learn what you can learn, do what you can do, and never give up hope!

The other thing, since I first introduced this in February 2004, is that not one person has ever asked me what I mean when I say, "Destiny comes to those who listen." I suppose they're assuming that the meaning is that destiny comes to those who listen to me which is certainly not the case.

The actual meaning is you must listen to your inner voice. It is your connection to God and the source of the wisdom you will need to explore your destiny. What destiny? Your destiny as a messenger of hope during what will be a dark and painful time for humanity as the Planet X system transits the inner core of our solar system.

If you search for your inner voice within and learn to listen to it with love and objectivity, you will know instinctively that while most of humanity will see this coming tribulation as a dark cloud, you will have the ability to see its silver lining and intuitively understand its meaning. What is coming is an un-shackling event. We, as a species, will be unshackled for we are slaves. Even though we will be dying and suffering in vast numbers, it is during this tribulation that we will do so as free men and women.

Therefore, your role as a survival wellness advocate is to help others see this silver lining and the hope for the future it portends; so they also will understand the need to preserve this fragile moment of freedom and thereby call the bluff, as we discussed in the first chapter.

Initially, your role will not be relevant to people who are in a state of panic. In my mind I see them racing up and down the aisles at box stores with loaded carts, screaming hysterically "Oh my God, they're out of Tabasco sauce were all going to die." For this reason you must be discreet when choosing to share your mission with others, this is the purpose of *Surviving the Planet X Tribulation: A Faith-Based Leadership Guide*. It is your bridging tool to building a relationship with those who will appreciate your mission.

Surviving the Planet X Tribulation

In *"Chapter 11 – Enlightened Continuity and Comfort"* I introduce the concept of *Survival Wellness Advocacy* to future survival community leaders:

> "So far we have talked about several roles in your community... but there is one special group of people in your community... This special group of people will be your survival wellness advocates, and they shall ensure the success of your strategy for enlightened continuity and comfort. Most will simply be called 'advocates' and the closest role model I can imagine for the role of an advocate would be the medicine men and women of Native American tribes."

This is why I say, "If you cannot afford a hill of beans, then you must be worth your weight in beans." As a survival wellness advocate, you are a sensitive in awareness and this is your destiny path. It is not your mission to finance bullets, beans, and bunkers. Others will be tasked with the responsibilities of making life possible. Your mission is to make life worth living.

Establishing your position within a faith-based survival community is a straightforward and simple process and it is explained on the back of the book under the heading, "For Those in Awareness:"

> "You are in awareness because God intends for you to be a part of the solution. Read and study this book thoroughly to prepare yourself for your true mission and calling. Then, when a spiritual leader you admire and respect is seeing the same clear and present danger that you are, your path is simple. Hand that leader this book as you say, 'You need a plan, and this is the plan that will work for what is coming. Please read it, and if you have any questions, I am always at your service.'"

"Are you worried for yourself and your loved ones because you cannot afford a mountain of beans? Then prove that you are worth your weight in beans by using this book as a bridging tool. It will help you to establish your value as a teacher, mentor, and comforter to those whom you are in service to."

"By reading and studying this book you'll experience firsthand the true power of the mentoring process. Then, when the time comes, be yourself as you mentor and comfort tribulation leaders through the difficulties of awareness compression. In this way you will gain their confidence, both through your centeredness and through your devotion to serving to others."

As a supplemental guide to *Surviving the Planet X Tribulation*, the purpose of this book, *Survival Wellness Advocacy*, is to give you, the Advocate, a deeper insight into your sacred mission. Because as a sensitive, you naturally see people holistically rather than myopically focusing just on their appearance, or what they say, and what they do. Yours is a world of intertwined subtleties that end with teachable moments of clarity. If this feels a bit overwhelming, it is time for you to take an inventory of your own destiny path.

Advocate Self-Assessment

If you are in awareness, there is no doubt that you have had a life filled with interesting adventures where you learned things and acquired skills for reasons other than having something to say on a job resume. Whether they were part of your wellness journey of discovery or a burr under your saddle, you've picked them up along the way.

As a survival wellness advocate, you need to reflect back on those experiences with a thoughtful self-assessment. You just might be surprised at how versatile you already are. For example, let's say you're a bookkeeper and you enjoy acting in Community Theater plays. When applying for a job, the accountant you're interviewing with will more likely be interested in your abilities to manage an accurate balance sheet then in your ability to play a leading role in a production of Auntie Mame.

However, during the tribulation, people who can grow beans will be more valued than those who can count them. Likewise, those who can engage members of the community with inspiring theatrical performances after they've scraped the last few beans off their plates will likewise be valued. Therefore, do not gauge the value of your life as an advocate in terms of economic ambitions.

Rather, use your precognitive powers to project yourself forward to a transitional time of great difficulty. This will be a time when your insights and life experiences will have prepared you as a teacher, a mentor, and comforter for those who survive the tribulation. It is also a time when many of those who do survive will envy the dead.

While preppers primarily focus their full attention and energy on the mundane business of bullets, beans, and bunkers they seldom if ever contemplate the despair. Each night, there will be those who eventually will lay their heads down to sleep and the prayer on their lips will be, "Dear God, I am so weary of this world and it's suffering. Please, please take me in my sleep."

If they are fortunate, God will hear their prayer and grant them their wish. But for the rest they will simply wake up in the morning and it will be another day of hardship, deprivations, impossible decisions, and more suffering. But what if God chose not to take them in their sleep, but rather, re-energize their will to survive?

In that case they will not wake up to find themselves in the misery of their lives. Instead they will wake to find you, their teacher, mentor, and comforter, and feel the gentle touch of your hand and warmth of your message to carry on with hope for the future.

To do this, you must be able to respond to a fundamental question, "Why is this happening?" If your answer is to shrug your shoulders, or to recite a thoughtful platitude you will fail as a survival wellness advocate. Therefore, it is imperative, that I now share with you, my answer to that pivotal question.

Why Is This
Happening?

In the upcoming tribulation many of the institutions that now define our present civilization are going to fail and at a dizzying pace. In a rapid staccato like succession ...ologies and ...isms will cease to have profound meaning as will many of our expectations. In that vacuum there will be a chaos that leaves us groping for something to hold onto.

Therefore, if you are to be truly effective as a survival wellness advocate, focusing on the reasons why our civilization collapsed will only keep you and those you attempt to help mired in the vacuum of the chaos. Where you need to focus is on how humanity can create a clean slate for the beginning of the next civilization. One that is enlightened and the pursuit of the acquisition of things which defines our present civilization is replaced by the pursuit of harmony. A harmony within ourselves and with all that is about us.

You must therefore be able to share a vision of this enlightened future. One cannot begin the pursuit of a victory unless they know what that victory will eventually look like. The key to enabling this vision must be rooted in a transcendent truth. The greatest truths are by and of necessity – simple. It is why the various mystery schools through which we seek a transcendent understanding weave us through years if not lifetimes of study simply to arrive at the great truth from which they are born.

However, during the tribulation, we will not have the luxury of the years, decades, or lifetimes to ponder mystery teachings. What is needed is a philosophy for the tribulation that can be easily grasped, and give to those who contemplate it a quick answer to the questions "what is creation and what is my role or function within it?"

It is for this reason that I was gifted with the insight that enables me to create a philosophy for survival during the tribulation and beyond. I call it "Perpetual Genesis."

Simply stated, the philosophy of Perpetual Genesis is based on three questions:

- Where does God live?
- What is God's mission?
- What is my role in God's mission?

You may note that the first question is not does God exist? That question always reminds me of the old joke about the German philosopher, Friedrich Nietzsche (1844-1900): "Nietzsche said God is dead. God said Nietzsche is dead." Frankly, I've always known and long felt my own personal relationship with God. It is not the kind of thing you need to beat your chest about for the entertainment of others. It is a quiet and humble knowing within.

Given that God does in fact exist, the answers to the three questions of Perpetual Genesis offer clarity and purpose that beleaguered tribulation survivors will need to prevail; answers that will satisfy the question, "Why is this happening?"

The History of Perpetual Genesis

As a survival wellness advocate, you are going to encounter a flood of experiences such as near-death, shared death, and out of body. Each of these is unique, but all three can be profound experiences. A profound experience of any kind occurs when the soul of the experiencer travels beyond the body and sees him or herself as an eternal being. In that profound moment the experiencer is forever changed. The extent of that change will vary between person and experience but there are three constants. He or she:

- Looses all fear of death.
- Looses interest in materialism.
- Gains a compelling desire to do good.

In my case, the tribulation philosophy of Perpetual Genesis was the direct result of a profound out of body experience decades ago.

As with the great truths at the core of mystery schools, this philosophy begins with a vision that requires the better part of a lifetime to understand. Its understanding may appear obvious at first; however, due to its possibilities and range of influence, it can boggle our mundane tunnel vision of existence. Therefore, one cannot truly appreciate the simplicity of a great truth from within the confines of the tunnel; rather, you must be free of it.

I left the confines of the tunnel when I was a young man in my mid-20s.

As the result of undisciplined paranormal experiences, I knew I needed a mentor. As the old adage goes, "When the student is ready, the teacher will appear" and this is what happened for me when my destiny path intersected that of a Native American medicine man.

His name was Hogue Lewis, and he had a gentle countenance. One that I often thought God had started with an ever-present warm smile and then pasted a man upon it. He took me under his wing and mentored me for many months in preparation for my vision quest.

When the day came that I knew where I wanted to have that experience, he knew that I was ready. So, I journeyed to the hills of Prescott, Arizona to a special place and there I had my vision quest. I traveled outside of my body and found myself in space, somewhere between earth and our sun. The earth was no larger than a basketball, and I could still feel the connection to my body, and I knew that I was in the presence of nurturing and loving spirits. In that instant I understood why those who have had profound experiences often report that they had no desire to return to their bodies because in that moment you realize how lonely and isolated we are in our physical incarnations.

I was then given a course of teachings, and while I was hovering in space I could see and understand them with perfect clarity. Yet, at the same time I knew that once I was back into my body it would take the better part of a lifetime for me to regain this clarity from within the confines of my limited physical being.

Likewise, I also knew that there would be a future event that would occur and awaken in me the eternal wisdom that had been shared with me that day so that I could share it with others.

You will recall in the first chapter that I shared with you my experience with Serapis Bey. What drove me to that event was the understanding that billions of people would die because they were engineered to that fate by self-serving elites bent on perpetuating their subjugation of our species beyond the tribulation.

To achieve their evil design, they not only needed to divide us and weaken us; they also needed to deprive us of the sense of who we are and where we fit in the scheme of things. In doing so, we would become easy prey to their schemes because they would then define our reality and our role in it in accordance with their own agendas.

However, once I vetted the channeled message of Serapis Bey, my life changed. This was the moment of epiphany I'd awaited since my vision quest in the hills of Prescott, Arizona the better part of a lifetime ago. I understood then that what I needed was to find my [S]ingle [P]oint [O]f [T]ruth, or "SPOT."

Imagine that you are working a large picture puzzle. After you dump the pieces out of the box and onto the table what is the first thing you do? You look for the four corners of the puzzle. Find them, and you know that every other piece of the puzzle is connected in some way to these four corner pieces. Ergo, the corners are your SPOT.

In my mind what I had been shown in my vision quest had become a box full of puzzle pieces and what I needed to do was to find my SPOT. This is when I formulated the three questions of Perpetual Genesis:

- Where does God live?
- What is God's mission?
- What is my role in God's mission?

Over the course of the next seven years, I reconnected the pieces with prayer, study, and meditation for one singular goal: To share a simple, greatest truth tribulation survivors could use to defeat the divisive and confusing manipulations of the elite.

Where Does God Live?

Traditional belief systems have what I call a line of sight or terrestrial view of God. That being, everything begins with the self and then expands outward to include family, community, church, nation, and so forth for as far as the eye can see or the mind can imagine. Beyond all of that is simply God; there is nothing beyond that. This is why the view is terrestrial.

However, the first question of Perpetual Genesis, "Where does God live?" is not based on a terrestrial view, but on a cosmic view. In other words, is there something beyond God?

During the 1980s, I was a science feature field producer for the Cable News Network, and at that time the holy grail of astronomy that received the lion share of all funding was Big Bang theory. I was also consumed by this question and for reasons I could not fathom at the time. Yet, I pursued this understanding with an unyielding personal conviction to possess the knowing of it.

Astronomers and scientists at that time were seeking to understand whether our universe was going to continue expanding until it disassembles itself in the vastness of the cosmos, or would gravity eventually reverse the expansion, and compress all that we know back into another singularity such as the one which first created us.

What science learned is we will not compress back into another singularity. This will not happen because that which is propelling the expansion of our universe is something which can only be understood through mathematics, dark energy. And dark energy is a powerful force indeed which happens to comprise approximately 68% of our universe.

Today, special interests use their government goons to suppress the research efforts of those seeking to create zero point energy devices to power our world. Their propagandists tell us that these inventors are trying to create perpetual motion contraptions in order to create energy. Everyone knows that perpetual motion contraptions though interesting in a Hollywood-esque way, are impossible. And this is very true.

So, what is the difference between zero point energy devices and perpetual motion contraptions? Apples and oranges.

To understand what a zero point energy device is and why it works, imagine the waveform of an oscilloscope. When presenting a waveform, the oscilloscope will give you the values for the waveform which will depend on what you're looking for. However, one value which does not change is zero. The waveform pattern will arch up into the positive (+) side of the values, then down through zero and into the negative (-) values, and then back up again as part of a continuous and repetitious waveform pattern.

At the zero point, the energy represented by the oscilloscope has no value. But what inventors have learned is that the zero point is a very special place. It is at the zero point value where the inventors can create a device that can extract, or pump if you will, dark energy.

This is why zero point inventions do not create something from nothing which is impossible. Rather, they tap into a vast source of cosmic energy at the zero point and siphon it out in usable form.

During the coming tribulation, we will see a whole new generation of Nikola Tesla's spring up, and free of the suppression of special interests and their government goons, they will gift us with new ways to power the new world and many other wondrous things. Believe it.

And herein is where we find the answer to the first question a Perpetual Genesis: "Where does God live?"

God lives in the void which is a combination of dark matter and dark energy. Together they comprise over 95% of all that there is and the baryonic or ordinary matter that we know and can see as our universe comprises less than 5%.

The void is infinite; whereas, the domain of God's creation is finite and small in comparison. The Big Bang did not occur as a result of some random event. It was the result of God's intention and it is through this intention that our universe came into being. However, if we are to assume that our universe is a one trick pony, is that not a childish, self-serving, and artificial limitation?

Rather, God lives within the void of dark energy and dark matter and is using this unlimited resource to create a multidimensional multi-verse of countless universes, each with its own physical laws. This is where God lives. And we live within that which God has manifested through intention.

This brings us to the second question.

What is God's Mission?

"To all things there is a purpose," is a given. What is not a given, is the reason for that purpose. For example, it could be happenstance, an accident, or the result of a noble purpose, a sense of mission in other words.

To presume that God created our universe by means of the Big Bang event simply out of loneliness for company is self flattery. An illogical and shortsighted terrestrial explanation we use like a child before a mirror painting her face with her mother's cosmetics for the first time. However, when we contemplate God's reason from a cosmic point of view, and we are standing far out in space and seeing the sun that lights our Earth as just another sparkle in the sky. Only then can we truly begin to appreciate the purpose by which we and our universe came into existence and to contemplate God's mission.

As I share with you my understanding of God's mission, please remember that the greatest truths are of necessity –simple.

God's Mission: The perpetual creation of life from the lifelessness of the void which is the ultimate expression of service to others.

This is the cornerstone of the tribulation philosophy of Perpetual Genesis, which now brings us to the third and final question and the discussion of need.

What Is My Role in God's Mission?

We turn to God often and for many reasons such as health, insight, and so forth. Various faiths offer a multitude of ways to ask for this help, but regardless of the reason or faith, the eventual purpose of these prayers is in most cases some form of service to self or for another.

Another way of looking at it is we, as eternal beings, are praying to God for help within the lifespan limitation of a single corporal incarnation. In other words we see our relationship with God on a terrestrial level as in "I am alive here, at this time, on this planet, incarnated in this species, and here is my immediate and specific need." While this terrestrial level view of our relationship with God is less than cosmic, God nonetheless helps us at this lower level.

Terrestrial vs. Cosmic View

The problems with seeing ourselves in a cosmic relationship with God are the manifestation of belief systems that admonish us that we only live once and that reincarnation does not exist. The fact is that these belief systems actually represent a minority of the human population on the planet at this time. They nevertheless are successful in pressing this view thanks to their immense economic and political power.

Why do they do this? One explanation is that exploring our relationship with God beyond the confines of the terrestrial view does expose us to certain risks, and we will discuss this at length later. The other is that this terrestrial limitation is stringently enforced since it serves the interests of those who anoint themselves as holy gatekeepers.

This is why those who have had profound out of body, shared death, and near death experiences so often find themselves at odds with the dogma and doctrine of checklist faiths. The reason why their experience is profound is that they lose their fear of death. The reason they lose their fear of death is due to the realization that reincarnation is how the universe works and always has. Consequently they ask questions that are not on the sanctioned questions lists, and because they go off list, they are often humiliated, mocked, and banished from their house of worship and study groups in the cruelest of ways.

Yet, the experience of seeing themselves as eternal beings and thereby losing their fear death is so powerful and unshakable that they refuse to yield to the intimidation and accept the banishment. Why? Because what they experienced connected them with God in a cosmic way and that transcends terrestrial beliefs. Therefore, while they may not embrace the philosophy of Perpetual Genesis, they will respect it as a noble path to the heart of a great mystery.

Those who do are very likely to be outcasts from the fringes of terrestrial faiths. They have the temerity and self-confidence to walk humbly with their God, and are on a path of their own choosing, in their own time, and in their own way. If this is you dear reader, then you are one step away from proclaiming your cosmic relationship with God, by saying "I am a Perpetual."

I Am a Perpetual

As a Perpetual, you are not pledging yourself to any belief system or institution of human creation. Rather, you reserve unto yourself the ultimate right of free will and your relationship with God which is solely determined by God and you and no other.

Why is free will the ultimate right? Because it is more precious than life itself, and there is a noble order to things. Without freedom we cannot responsibly master our power of free will as God wants for each of us. This is because freedom is the foundation of free will; free will is the energizing force of intention; and intention is the power to create universes.

This is why with the philosophy of Perpetual Genesis we embrace our relationship with God on the cosmic level and say:

> "God, as an eternal being, I am in service to your mission of perpetually creating life from the lifelessness of the void. I am presently incarnated here at this time, on this planet, in this species, and in service to your mission. When my work here is completed, I pledge myself to you as an eternal being to continue being in service to your mission in the next incarnation, time, planet and species of your choosing. I am forever with you."

When you accept this eternal responsibility to exercise your free will in service to others, your relationship with God will transcend the terrestrial level to the cosmic level, and God will assist you privately and personally with an eternal service to others sense of empowerment.

This is why I founded the Knowledge Mountain Church of Perpetual Genesis in 2015. It is not to tell you how to walk humbly with your God; for that would be the ultimate disrespect of your free will. For this reason, our church frowns on proselytizing through persuasive or coercive means to induce others away from what are regarded as inferior or misleading beliefs. To inform is noble; to persuade or coerce is not.

Our mission is to help you come together with like-minded others who also seek the noble sense of mission that comes with the rising up from the corporal limitations of the terrestrial level in your personal relationship with God to the eternal cosmic level in service to God's mission of Perpetual Genesis.

This commitment is a burden to contemplate, but it's a new freedom to experience, and so few will take this eternal pledge. It is my hope that if you choose not to that you will respect those who have.

The Struggle for Freedom

The book, *Surviving the Planet X Tribulation: A Faith-Based Leadership Guide*, explains the coming Planet X tribulation events, threats, and tactics at the leadership level. However, the overarching goal of the book is to offer a noble reason for the survival and the freedom of our species.

Therefore, let us revisit the wisdom of Serapis Bey. As was mentioned previously, the story of humankind is an immense and unfinished book of many chapters, and this present chapter which is soon coming to a close, belongs to the elites. However, the next chapter of life belongs to us provided we are ready to seize it.

As a Survival Wellness Advocate, or someone who employs part or all of the mission teachings, there is an acronym you need to understand immediately about the dark side which exists on many planes of existence, (M)ethodical, (P)aced, and (P)ersistent.

Therefore, let us begin with what the dark side, through the agency of the elites, has done to set us up for failure during the coming tribulation. Their goal being that we will be so divided and weak that when they emerge from their underground lairs with the inducements of their bluff, the remaining survivors will feebly succumb and thereby re-shackle countless generations to come under the yoke of slavery.

Setup for Failure

There are physical signs of what the elites are doing to weaken us: such as geoengineering (chemtrails), GMO foods, fluoridation, pesticides, forced immunizations, fracking, nuclear generating plants, and the list goes on. Each of these things are setting us up for a time when life will be more difficult and when our bodies, which have been weakened through overuse of antibiotics in the food chain, will be far more susceptible to deadly afflictions than those living in the Third World.

To some extent, there are ways that we can address the attacks upon us to destroy our physical resiliency. Thankfully, our bodies are very good at healing themselves, provided we give them a chance. However, there is a crisis of resiliency that is far more pernicious is what the elites are doing to weaken us physically.

Case in point is what we now know as the Snowflake Generation or Generation Snowflake, sometimes referred to as the "poor loser generation." The young American adults of our present time, they are called Snowflakes because of their fragility. Like snowflakes in our environment, they can only exist in perfect conditions. For example, a snowflake can only reach the ground if the air temperatures are below freezing from where they are formed all the way to the ground. In other words, snowflakes are not resilient to changes in their environment.

With this in mind, imagine it is December 7, 1941. In a matter of days, America will become engaged in a world war on two fronts and that the only manpower resource available is mostly comprised of young, snowflake generation adults. In that case, could we win the war or will we become the spoils of the Axis powers, with their determined generations of adults seeking global domination?

What we need to understand is that Snowflakes were not born fragile. They were made fragile by the elites. Remember MPP: Methodical, paced and patient. Since the Vietnam War era, there has been a succession of subtle changes, methodically programmed by our educational and political systems to produce political correctness and a culture of victimization. Now everyone can find a way to be victimized. Minorities who once lived at the fringes of society are now the victims of society and strangely enough, the majorities who oppress them have in turn become victims of the minority.

Those of my age can remember an education system that focused on reading, writing and arithmetic and preparing us to be productive, self-sufficient, thinking people. Likewise, it centered our lives on God and our nation each morning we recited the pledge of allegiance and prayed together. It was a time when only 10% of marriages failed and young adults took pride in moving out of the family home as soon as they could to make a life of their own. And it was a time when a child from a modest working class family could afford a college education without being saddled by usurious debt.

Today, over half of all marriages fail and we now have a dependent generation saddled by you service student loans and a broken promise of jobs who now find it easier to move back in with their parents than to make they own independent way. When I was a young man I had a choice about my economic future. But today, we have young adults saddled with slave debt for college educations that are no longer in demand and their choice is simple. Live forever at the poverty level as the interest compounds at a vicious so their student debts perpetually force them to remain in poverty, or, win the lottery.

The point here is that this shows us just one of the many ways the elites have methodically implemented a paced and persistent strategy to divide the populous so that we're no longer objective thinkers. Rather, more of us than ever before are dependent and prone to emotional, hair-trigger confrontations.

Everyone who teaches business negotiation techniques begins by telling their students, that you have to see things from the other side of the table. You need to see how the person you are negotiating with views you and your offer and what that means. So let's apply the same logic to the elites.

Their agenda is to perpetuate the enslavement of our species following the tribulation, so imagine that you know what is coming, and that this tribulation event will destroy your control mechanisms.

For a brief period of a few years, people will be dying in the billions, but they will be dying as free humans. Should the slaves, acquire a taste for the freedom at this time, your chances of bluffing them back into slavery will be shattered.

Given this, who would you want to see on the other side of the table?

Would you want to see a more-independent, spiritually-oriented populace, such as the one that fought and prevailed in the dark days of World War II? Or, would you want to see dependent Snowflakes that are socially divided victims, prone to knee-jerk emotional responses and therefore easy to control?

So what does this mean for you? If you are going to become a member of a survival community, you will be going down into the bunkers with the snowflakes and the pressures of surviving the tribulation will result in a non-stop crisis of young adults acting out their hysterical dramas. Not because these young adults were born to do this. They were made to do this by an evil agenda.

With that in mind, harken to the wisdom of an old saying, "What is sauce for the goose is sauce for the gander." In other words, you too can employ the (M)ethodical, (P)aced, and (P)ersistent strategy, with great effect. There are no one trick pony solutions here. You will need to follow this strategy each and every day, no matter how repetitive it may feel. Remember, the dark side is very comfortable with repetition and so must you, if you are to successfully pursue your sacred mission.

Your Sacred Mission

As a Survival Wellness Advocate, it is difficult to look at the vast array of techniques and resources available to the elites for their evil aims and to maintain some sense of hope. But no matter what we do in the end, they will prevail. If you are feeling this, then take heart for those willing to stand for freedom have three distinct advantages that are beyond the reach of the elites and therefore despised and feared by them: Critical mass, healing power and God's plan.

Critical Mass

The elites fear our numbers because if we mobilize, we will overwhelm them. A good example of this was Operation Barbarossa, the Nazi invasion of the Soviet Union on Sunday, 22 June 1941. The Nazis easily overran and destroyed much of Stalin's Army and Air Force facing them. But Russia regrouped and came back at the German's with considerable force and overwhelmed them. The observation of Wehrmacht Colonel Bernd Von Kielst best sums it up:

> "The German Army in fighting Russia is like an elephant attacking a host of ants. The elephant will kill thousands, perhaps even millions, of ants, but in the end their numbers will overcome him, and he your ears it was yours will be eaten to the bone."

The point here, enough survivors stand up for their freedom, the plans of the elites to perpetuate their slavery of the planet afar the tribulation will fail. Is a majority required? No.

During the American Revolution, 70% of the colonists either sat on the sidelines or sided with the British and yet 30% of the colonists were able to win the war. In other words, defeating the subjugation plans of the elite will not require a majority of survivors just enough to call the bluff.

When the elites offer their inducements to slavery, courageous freedom-loving people will know they are not saying "no" to the carrot. They're saying "no" to the stick and it will strike them with a terrible vengeance. Yet, all it will take will be enough such courageous souls to achieve a critical mass, and then the weight of humanity will crush down upon the elites and humankind will enter an enlightened age of true freedom.

Healing Power

When one considers the complexity of extensive planning, funding, development and operation of the elitist schemes to dumb us down and to cheat us of our natural health, the vast scope of these evil endeavors leave us wondering if we can overcome the hurdles set in our path in time to survive the coming tribulation.

But this is the way of the elites. They will not only tell us where they are strong and where we are weak, they will be sure to amplify the perception of their strengths. That being said, what they do not want us to know is our strengths and so they shout over us to suppress our own ability to see within.

We have many strengths, but the one they fear and revile the most is the healing power of God's love. This is the one thing the elites will never be able to stop nor derive benefit from. Conversely, when you are attending holistically to the mine bodies and souls of your survival community members, this is the first thing you must always reach for when you open your first aid kit.

Where there is a will, there is a way and there are many simple things that can be done to restore natural health to our minds, emotions bodies and souls. In the doing of this, you will undo the elitist weakening of the populace and it will hamper their power over us no differently then shattering the clanking tracks of a tank. Mired in the mud, the extent of its harm becomes limited and it becomes vulnerable.

God's Plan

In the previous chapter *Why Is This Happening?* You learned about God's Mission, the perpetual creation of life from the lifelessness of the void. So, if you as a Perpetual have pledged your eternal soul to this mission, the natural question is what is the plan? For if one is to enjoy success as the old saying goes, one must "plan the work and work the plan." Therefore, what is God's plan and how do we fit into it.

If we want to understand God's noble thinking, we need only see it reflected in our noble thinking, for in a manner of speaking, our noble virtues like the golden spiral of nature's numbering system represented within the Nautilus shell. Known as Fibonacci numbers, this system appears everywhere in Nature, such as the leaf arrangement in plants and the scales of a pineapple.

With this metaphor in mind, we ask, "how is enlightenment expressed through our noble virtues?" For that, one must remember that America is a nation of immigrants. Hard-pressed people, who were drawn to the freedom and opportunity of America, left their homelands and crossed the oceans in the steerage of steamships. They were the opportunists and predators to be sure, but the vast majority of them were honest people with the dream.

They knew they would have hard and brutal lives working 12 hours a day in steamy unsafe sweatshops and enduring the deprivations of cramped, cold water flats where eight families would share a single toilet. Yet, what gave them the moral strength to endure the hardships was a dream. That their children would learn to become accountants, lawyers, college professors and the such so their grandchildren could become violinists and opera singers and thereby bring a few moments of beauty to an otherwise difficult world.

To achieve this, a system of education was necessary, beginning with grammar schools, than middle schools, high schools colleges and eventually, institutions of higher learning. Now let us use this as a metaphor for the golden spiral of God's plan.

Theologians will often tell us that the body is a vessel for the soul. Yet when you communicate with enlightened spirits across the other side of the veil, they never use the term vessel. They always use the term vehicle. So what is the difference?

A vessel is something that must be placed and organized in relationship to other vessels by an external force. Namely that of a theological gatekeeper. On the other hand, a vehicle is a vessel with wheels. It is designed to go where ever the soul within it chooses.

The purpose of our vessels is for our souls to physically incarnate and search for wisdom and discipline to master free will. Like the children and grandchildren of a poor hard-working immigrant, are souls evolve and must therefore require more sophisticated environments with each incarnation. Therefore, the question becomes, what does evolution and enlightenment look like?

On a physical level we change in response to our environment. But for the purpose of enlightenment we change in a way that is unobservable to the naked eye. To understand this, let us examine the assumption that God's plan for us is that we are to become more like roses so that more enlightened souls, those further along, we'll be able to incarnate in corporal vehicles capable of offering them the necessary environment.

At present the vibrational frequency of a healthy human body ranges anywhere from 62 to 78Hz, which limits our species' ability as mortal vessels to host the more spiritually advanced and higher-vibrating souls.

Conversely, why is it we give roses as expressions of our love and sympathy, despite their prickly thorns? After all, being pricked by a Rose thorn is not an enjoyable experience. Yet we value them in a very special way. It is because the vibrational frequency of a rose is 320Hz, the highest vibrational rate available to us in all of nature.

For this reason, even the slowly dying Roses delivered by our florists, can sustain an emotionally nurturing vibrational rate.

Simply stated, God's plan for humanity is to increase our vibrational rate so that we can serve as corporal vessels for more ascended spirits. In doing so, our species can offer a pathway for the ascension of the spiritual masters who will incarnate among us. These ascended spiritual masters will in turn be able to serve God's mission of Perpetual Genesis in a very special way.

To visualize this, imagine that you are holding a warm bottle of champagne. Now shake it vigorously, place it on the table and pop the cork. What happens next is that a powerful foam of many bubbles issues forth from the top of the bottle down along the sides and onto the table.

Imagine the champagne bottle as God and that each of bubble foaming out of the neck of the bottle is a unique universe unto itself, with its own physical laws. Because the bottle represents God, it endlessly converts the limitless dark energy and dark matter of the void in Big Bangs bubbles. This is why God's plan for us as a species is to serve as teaching vessels for Ascended Masters, who in turn will eventually create the bubbles within the foam.

This brings us to the reason why the dark side on its many planes of existence does all the evil it does. Instead of helping to create the champagne foam of the multi-verse, they want to steal it and enjoy it without investing even the smallest of noble effort. And this brings us to the crux of the tribulation.

Why The Tribulation?

The reason why the dark spirits are so effective in their ability to interfere with us and to suppress our own evolution as corporal vessels for ascended souls is that our current vibrational level is limited to a range of 62 to 78Hz.

If as a species our vibrational frequency increases substantially so that we may be corporal vessels for ascended Masters, then our higher vibrational frequency will put us out of their reach, thereby denying them a valuable food source.

You see, we can debate the motives to the dark side on its various planes of existence, until the cows come home and still miss the point. They are parasites and they need to feed on our life force energy. No matter how convoluted our thinking, all that the dark side does is cast us into a state of fear, because this is when they can milk us like life force energy sows and the greater and more intense the fear, the more we nourish their parasitic needs.

Are you wondering why it is they need to feed on us like parasites? If so consider this, there are only two directions an entity can travel. It is either towards the light of God's love or away from it towards the cold, inky blackness of oblivion. When we travel towards God we are gifted with life force energy and without life force energy, all entities will inevitably sink into oblivion and therein be rewarded with death eternal. So the dark side must steal that which it refuses to gather by advancing into the light of God's love.

This is why the dark side favors subjugation over freedom, because as a free species we can follow God's plan and increase our vibrational rate. Remember, freedom is the foundation of free will and free will is the energizing force of intention and intention is the power to create universes.

So what can you as an individual survival wellness advocate do to be in service to God's plan? The first step is to imagine the parasites of the dark side in your mind as you say, "Let them eat vacuum."

"OK, you say, 'how is this done?'" The answer is simple.

Break The Cycle

In the coming tribulation, humanity must once and for all break the cycle of Empire which is based upon acquisition, greed and exploitation. It is why all empires fail, because they rise quickly while as there is enough to go around, but as elites consolidate the resources and political power of the Empire into their own hands, they simultaneously drain it of vitality. Consequently, a greatly weakened body politic will invariably succumb to a minor challenge it could have handily overcome in its early.

The result is that shell that was once a vibrant Empire collapses like a house of straw.

Therefore, we must move beyond the failed strategies of empires of acquisition to a new paradigm of harmony instead of acquisition. Harmony within ourselves and all that is about us. This is what God's plan has on offer for us, and if we are willing to seize that which is ours, we will rise beyond the parasitic manipulations of the dark side, thorough a harmonious state that will naturally come with a higher vibrational rate. This is why freedom is a natural desire that time and again, our courageous ancestors have shown us to be more precious than life itself.

Freedom is a Natural Desire

Fear and love are the real difference between God's plan and the parasitic feeding needs of the dark side.   To unleash the power of fear, energy must be invested. To unleash the power of love, energy must be released.

As a sensitive and in awareness, you have three responsibilities: to be a teacher, a mentor, and a comforter. Regardless whether you embrace any part or all of the philosophy of Perpetual Genesis, these responsibilities nonetheless remain yours as a sensitive in awareness.

The Three Precepts

I founded the Knowledge Mountain Church of Perpetual Genesis in 2015 upon the following three precepts:

- **Self-Sufficiency:** Independence is the foundation of spiritual freedom. Spiritual freedom gives the ability to advance toward ascension, as well as the ability for our species as a whole to evolve spiritually.

- **Hope for the Future:** While others will lament the end of this civilization, we see a new beginning, a clean slate for the creation of the next civilization. We believe in a more enlightened future for all of us, everywhere.

- **Knowing you are Not Alone:** Those long in awareness, and those newly coming into awareness, are a thinly spread minority. Yet, we are a minority that is growing larger each day.

Every teaching of our Church is based on these three precepts. So let's assume you choose to identify yourself as a Perpetual, with the three responsibilities of awareness, so we can see how they align with the three precepts of our Church.

The Three Precepts	Awareness Responsibilities	Survival Wellness Advocate
Self-Sufficiency	Teaching	The most immediate need of any survival community will be a natural program of holistic health that encompasses the mind body and spirit. As an advocate you will invest significant amount of time in teaching wellness techniques and practices. For example, giving classes in hygiene and self-healing energy arts like Yoga and Danjeon Breathing.
Hope for the Future	Mentoring	While hope for the future needs to be encouraged at all levels of leadership, as an advocate you will spend your time working with individuals or families in a mentoring role, where you are responding to their individual concerns for the future.
Knowing You are Not Alone	Comforting	The worst place for a person to be during the tribulation, will be a lonely place. As an Advocate, you will need to continually reinforce the feeling that people are a valuable member of the community. Likewise, people also need to know that they are part of something bigger than themselves that is noble and worthy of their passion and attention.

Never forget, you are an Advocate. It is not your role to be political. Rather, stay focused on your three responsibilities, along with the three precepts if you so choose. Then you will unleash the natural desire of freedom that resides within each and every one of us.

Succeed in this, by helping people to enjoy wellness and to feel hope and purpose, and you will remove the shackles that bind them to slavery. Then, they will do what comes naturally as countless generations before us have done pursue freedom.

In the next part of the book, Survival Wellness, we will examine the more practical aspects of your role in helping people to experience wellness so that they can appreciate freedom.

Part 2 – Survival Wellness

First Contact

As a Survival Wellness Advocate, your mission is to serve your community and its leaders in three roles: teacher, mentor, and comforter. To be successful, you must be spiritually and emotionally centered because you must be the eye of the storm that is coming. This is essential when you present yourself to the community's leadership and then to its membership at large.

When catastrophic events begin to unfold, they will be extremely unsettling for everyone. While some will be caught up by the events they are completely unprepared for, many will respond in ways that are self-destructive, and you will see the truth of what needs to be done. From the outset you must demonstrate courage and the strength of your convictions to take effective action and guide others into taking action along with you.

In this manner the leaders you first contact and their members, once you have established a role in the community, will come to see you in much the same way as sailors, when they are tossed in the tumult of a hurricane, find calm in the eye of the storm. Peace and calm, while all about them is madness.

Think of the leader of the community like the captain of the ship, and the members his crew. Everyone on a storm-tossed vessel will see and take comfort from your being calm and centered, but the one who will value you most will be the vessel's captain. It will be the captain who will ask you, "What is the meaning of all this?" and, "What do we need to do now?" Not out of fear or desperation, but to access the calm, wise decisions needed for the benefit of all the souls aboard that good ship.

Even for the captain, this will be a storm such as none have ever seen before. But you have had the knowing of this storm through your dreams, visions, and premonitions.

Leadership First Contact

So, where and when will you board this good ship and come to be known and valued by its captain?

I give the answer to this on the back cover of my new book, *Surviving the Planet X Tribulation: A Faith-Based Leadership Guide,* in the following message to sensitives and those in awareness:

"Know this — you are in awareness because God intends for you to be a part of the solution. Your role is to be a mentor, a comforter, and a teacher during the tribulation. Read and study this book thoroughly to prepare yourself for your true mission. Then, when a spiritual leader you admire and respect is seeing the same clear and present danger that you are, your path is simple. Hand that leader this book as you say, 'You need a plan, and this is the plan that will work for what is coming. Please read it, and if you have any questions, I am always at your service.'"

"By reading and studying this book you'll experience firsthand the true power of the mentoring process. Then, when the time comes, be yourself as you mentor and comfort tribulation leaders through the difficulties of awareness compression. In this way you will gain their confidence, both through your centeredness and through your devotion to serving to others."

As any good negotiator will tell you, you must always see things from the other side of the table. So, how does this apply to your first contact with the leader of a survival community?

One thing you can certainly count on is that these people will be surrounded by those unprepared for this coming storm, and they will act out in a swirling, angry pattern of shock, anger, denial, and every other form of fear-based emotion imaginable.

For a wise leader of a community, the mantle of responsibility will force them to cut through the fog of fear; they will understand the destructive consequences of these out-of-control emotions and the need to be calm in the midst of the storm.

A leader will perceive your strength based in your awareness and service to others as a place of calm in the eye of the storm. Your awareness of truth born of unconditional love and service to others is better able to assess the situation, formulate a plan, and then take action on that plan, even if it is not the most optimal plan.

This is the whole underlying strategy of my new book, *Surviving the Planet X Tribulation: A Faith-Based Leadership Guide.* It is designed to give those in awareness a clear path to find the calm in the eye of the storm; to be that calm voice of reason during the tribulation, and thereby become valued members of faith-based survival communities.

It is for this very reason that if you are going to be a truly effective Survival Wellness Advocate, you must acquire not one but two copies of this book. One is for the leader you will approach to serve; the other you will keep studying intensively for it will demonstrate to you the mentoring process that will make you invaluable to the leadership of a survival community. So, let's take a look at the part of the book that establishes your value as a teacher, mentor and comforter.

In *"Chapter 11 – Enlightened Continuity and Comfort"* I introduce the concept of *Survival Wellness Advocacy* to future survival community leaders:

> "So far we have talked about several roles in your community... but there is one special group of people in your community... This special group will be your survival wellness advocates, and they shall ensure the

success of your strategy for enlightened continuity and comfort. Most will simply be called 'advocates' and the closest role model I can imagine for the role of an advocate would be the medicine men and women of Native American tribes."

This is why I say, "If you cannot afford a hill of beans, then you must be worth your weight in beans." As a survival wellness advocate, you are a sensitive in awareness and this is your destiny path. It is not your mission to finance bullets, beans, and bunkers. Others will be tasked with the responsibilities of making life possible. Your mission is to make life worth living.

Once you have established a working relationship with the leader, or leadership of the survival community, half of the job is done. The other half requires that you establish a working relationship with the members of the community. But first, we need to establish an essential ground rule.

Doctors Cure – Advocates Help

Doctors have patients because their job is to get sick people well. Good old-fashioned critical care, if you will. But as a survival wellness advocate you have clients because your job is survival wellness. You help to keep healthy survivors healthy with a holistic approach encompassing mind, body, and soul.

This is why the one word you will never hear me say is "cure," and by the way, neither should you. Only doctors cure. Advocates help, but not only their clients, they help doctors as well by reducing their crisis care workload. This helps them by giving them more time for education, research, and the creation of medicines and instruments.

That being said, sometimes things get hectic. When that happens and the community doctor tells you to clean and dress a wound, you jump right to it because first and foremost you are a caring and loving member of that community. Do your best and never, never, never say the "can't" word. If you have a question, ask it and if you get squeamish, deal with it and get the job done.

However, on a day-to-day basis, you'll come into face-to-face contact with most community members, and over time they will become your extended wellness family. In the process, you'll work on an informal clinical care basis, teaching energy healing classes, administering essential oils and so forth.

Membership First Contact

When you approach the members of a survival community for the first time and announce that you're a survival wellness advocate, the first thing you'll likely hear is "say what?" Therefore, they will need to know what differentiates you as a survival wellness advocate, from other roles such as physicians, ham radio operators and gunsmiths. Vocations they'll automatically understand.

Because wellness advocacy will be a new concept for them, it is imperative that you quickly and confidently establish your value to the community members above and beyond your value to their leadership.

Your primary vocation focus will be on disease prevention for this reason, because during a tribulation, communicable diseases will claim the lives of more survivors than any other single cause. This is why you need to promote yourself as a community superbug fighter, with an arsenal of time-tested, natural, simple, safe and effective immune system aids and survival skills.

You must show at this point versatility in your skill set, and you must engage the community members in a pleasing, experiential way. First, let's talk about versatility, which means helping people with a wide range of problems.

As an example, imagine that you walk into a community and say, "Everything I know, I learned by finding a natural way to treat my own Problemitis. So if you've got a problem with Problemitis, I'm your Problemitis expert. That's what I do."

Do this and the members will look at each other and say, "Anybody here got Problemitis?" If everyone shrugs their shoulders, you're a one trick pony. Thank you and goodbye.

On the other hand if you said something like, "I've taught myself how to deal with common survival needs such as immune system support, dust storm sinus headaches, bunker stress, menstrual cramps, low back pain, and much more with natural solutions." Now you've used versatility to start a serious conversation, but folks may still remain unclear about what you do.

Here is where you will need to build confidence, perceived value, and have powerful first contact tools that you can carry in your pocket, essential oils. Since this is a first contact situation, the fastest way for people to appreciate what you can do for them is to feel it, and in this regard nothing works better or faster than essential oils.

Essential Oils for First Contact

The reason why essential oils are critical to your success as an Advocate is that they have a Biblical history of success. However, for the more science-minded survivalists, you need to tell them that you only use therapeutic grade essential oils that are safe and made for maximum potency, purity, and shelf life.

With that the first oil you'll pull out of your pocket is Lavender. Open a vial and put a few drops on everyone's palms and demonstrate how to use it. When making first contact, here is how I would explain it.

"There will be times when everyone must spend time in the bunker together. Tornadoes, wind storms, ash clouds, hail storms, meteorite showers and so forth. When that happens, things will get cramped and likewise difficult for bathing. That's why I call Lavender essential oil, the bunker blossom."

With that have a few folks hold out one hand, palms up and put one or two drops of Lavender on their palm. As a note of caution, advise them not to operate machinery after this experience. Then instruct them to rub their palms together and then have them hold their palms up to their face so they can smell the oil as they inhale.

As they do, ask them to think about what they're feeling after rubbing this oil into their hands and inhaling it. Then after a few minutes, ask them if they are feeling calmer and more at peace, and if they like the oil's pleasant odor.

When they tell you that they're feeling more relaxed and their moods have improved, let them know, by putting several drops of Lavender oil into a low-power atomizer, the whole bunker will become pleasantly infused. This will help with annoying odors, ease stress, and tension for a more restful environment.

Here is also where a little humor is a good thing. Put on a bright smile and say something like, "and like they say on television, but wait there is more."

Next you produce a vial of Lemon essential oil and tell them that this oil can also help keep spirits up. This is because Lemon is a great way to cleanse the air and uplift mood in the cramped confines of a bunker plus, it complements other essential oils, like Lavender. Then put a drop on everyone's other palm and have them smell it alone. Then instruct them to rub their palms together so they can smell how nicely it blends with the Lavender they've just experienced.

Another essential oil you want to use for first contact is Peppermint. Open the vial and let them smell it. A huge benefit of Peppermint is its global familiarity as a scent.

Here is where you can drop a little factoid that really demonstrates knowledge depth. For example, you could tell them that one drop of therapeutic grade essential peppermint oil is as effective as 28 cups of peppermint tea.

This is why Peppermint will be one of the essential oils that you'll administer most to counter the effects of what I call the plague foods. These are GMO plants mutated with animal genes.

They are alien to our bodies and saturated with poisonous chemicals which now are sprayed on crops just before harvest.

In a diet which is solely dependent on these packaged and canned GMO death foods, such as spaghetti, mac and cheese, and so forth, survivors will experience lethargy, depression, impaired thinking and a whole range of gastrointestinal issues such as acid stomach, diarrhea and gas.

The worse hit will be the very young and the very old, so expect that some members of the community already will be experiencing GMO plague food symptoms. Rub two drops of Peppermint essential oil on their bellies and watch as they feel the difference.

As you can see, studying the *Surviving the Planet X Tribulation: A Faith-Based Leadership Guide* and *learning about simple resources like* essential oils can give you a huge, first contact advantage in presenting yourself as valuable to the leadership and members of a faith-based survival community.

A Look Ahead

Part two of this book focuses on the day-to-day activities and demands you'll face as a Survival Wellness Advocate.

- **Environmental and Radiation Threats:** in addition to all of the expected threats we'll face during the tribulation, there will be new ones both natural and man-made that you must help community leaders and members anticipate.

- **Mental and Emotional Support:** of all the important things you are going to do, this will be the most important and it will demand more of your time and emotional strength than anything else.

- **Primary Modalities:** These are things you'll do every day to keep healthy survivors healthy.

◢ **Secondary Modalities:** These are the tools and techniques you'll use in conjunction with the primary modalities, on an as-needed basis.

◢ **Energy Healing Arts:** There is a vast array of self-healing energy arts, but the ones best suited to the demands of tribulation survival will require a minimum amount of floor space and calories.

◢ **Related Advocacy Skills**: These are additional skills you can acquire to enhance your value to the community. For example, taking a Red Cross course on adult and pediatric first aid and CPR.

◢ **Forming a Guild:** The ideal size for community is 100 members or more, with five or more advocates. For this reason the advocates need to form a Guild, as soon as possible.

Remember, the goal of part two of this book is to introduce you to a range of issues, skills, and resources. These chapters will provide a framework upon which you can expand your research and your efforts to create your own robust set of valuable advocate skills.

Environmental and Radiation Threats

In Chapter 7 of *Surviving the Planet X Tribulation: A Faith-Based Leadership Guide,* a tribulation threat matrix pyramid is presented with the following six levels, ranked by deadliness:

- Space
- Earth
- Industrial
- Weather
- Water
- Health

The premise of the threat matrix is an inverse relationship between the threats and their level of importance. Therefore, more attention is paid to the level of Health which forms the base of the pyramid than the levels above it. The logic being that the threats you can do most to mitigate are likely to be more frequent and pervasive and therefore deserve the greatest efforts.

A plethora of the threats and their various levels are discussed in the book. However, in order to illustrate for you the issues that you as a survival wellness advocate will need to address, the effects of geoengineering (chemtrail) spraying, volcanic ash and solar radiation must be considered.

Geoengineering Spraying (Chemtrails)

The Internet is filled with videos showing jets at an altitude of approximately 20 to 25,000 feet spraying chemicals. The elites have the populace convinced that these are condensation trails and that there is no such thing as chemtrails. This is a terrible and horrible lie.

Next time you go to the airport and you're waiting in the passenger lounge for your flight to board, gaze out the window at the airplanes you see parked at the ramps and pay close attention to their engines. Notice how the front end of these engines has a bulbous shape. Then look at the narrow tube protruding from the rear of the engine.

What you see is called a high bypass jet engine and these have been used by commercial jetliners for decades because they reduce noise pollution and are more fuel-efficient.

The bulbous shape at the front is the bypass fan cowling that directs air through and around the turbine engine. Only a fraction of the air that enters the engine through the front is taken in by the turbine engine. The rest passes around the turbine engine, or bypasses it if you will. Consequently what comes out of the back of the engine is a mixture of hot and cold air.

These types of engines can only produce contrails under very specific conditions, such as flying through the humid skies near the equator. The jets that do produce contrails will either be military or private jets which can use pure jet engines.

This is important to keep in mind because as you look at these different jets, private versus commercial, notice the contrails that follow behind the small private jets. They do not go across the sky; they dissipate quickly. Conversely, when you see large commercial aircraft with high bypass jet engines producing contrails that not only cross the sky but also persist for a long time, you are seeing the chemicals that are sprayed on us each and every day. The fact is these geoengineering jets crisscross the globe spraying 20 million tons of toxic metals a year into the stratosphere.

What they spray is a witch's brew of many toxic metals but chief among them is aluminum. While aluminum occurs naturally in the environment, it lacks the purity of the man-made aluminum which is being sprayed.

The reason given for the spraying is to provide a sun shield to create what is called "solar dimming." This is why climate models are in chaos. On the one hand we know that carbon and methane is going into the atmosphere and creating a greenhouse effect known as global warming. Yet, on the other hand we are seeing lower temperatures at the same time. So what are the results today?

- While Alzheimer's disease is officially listed as the sixth-leading cause of death in the United States, the fact is that one third of all seniors dying today, have some form of Alzheimer's and Dementia.

- Bee populations are collapsing and not only in farm areas where pesticides and cell phone tower radiation are blamed. They're dying in the wild as well, far away from pesticides and cellular radiation. This is a real concern for humanity because in the words of physicist Albert Einstein, "If the bee disappeared off the surface of the globe, then man would have only four years of life left. No more bees, no more pollination, no more plants, no more animals, no more man."

- Autism has become a 21st century pandemic. In 2000, 1 in 150 newborns were autistic. Today that ratio has more than doubled to 1 in 68. Even worse, at the present rate of spraying, half of all newborns born in 2030 will be autistic.

What all three of these outcomes have in common is the aluminum that is used in geoengineering spraying programs. As a survival wellness advocate, there are two aspects of this we need to discuss. First, can you do anything about it? And then, what is the social programming significance of this?

Mitigating Chemtrail Aluminum

The problem with chemtrailing is that aluminum now is pervasive throughout the environment, so as a survival wellness advocate your focus needs to be on ways to help the body eliminate excess aluminum.

When a community is making choices for what it is going to stockpile and eventually grow to feed itself, there are things you can do. In terms of stockpiling avoid aluminum cans and processed food packaging. It is better to purchase organic foods that can store for long periods of time, and to pack them yourselves in sealed buckets.

One, of the things people will be using quite a bit during the tribulation, is antacids. Here, you can read the labels to make a difference. Avoid brands that use aluminum hydroxide and magnesium carbonate, such as Gaviscon, Maalox and Mylanta, in favor of brands that use calcium carbonate such as Rolaids and Tums. Better yet, good old-fashioned sodium bicarbonate tablets and powder get the job done quite nicely.

Another way to help mitigate aluminum is to detoxify your body with a gentle colon cleanse such as Perfect 7. I've personally used it for years, and found it to be a super duper pooper mover.

Turmeric has become quite popular in America for wellness, and it also happens to be useful in helping the body to eliminate aluminum as well. However, one of the best things you can do is to drink silica-rich mineral water. The amount of silica in the different brands varies, but the one with the most amount of silica is Fiji.

Another way to get the aluminum elimination benefit of silica is to stockpile and grow foods that are naturally high in silica. Below is the short list to illustrate the point:

- Oats, 100g – 595mg
- Millet 100g – 500mg
- Barley 100g – 233mg
- Potatoes 100g – 200mg
- Red beets 100g – 21mg
- Asparagus 100g – 18mg
- Green beans (cooked), 250g – 6.10mg
- Carrot (raw, peeled), 200g – 4.58mg
- Brown rice, 200g – 4.14mg

Even if the geoengineering spraying program ends early into the major events of the tribulation, there are two other aspects that need to be discussed: "Chemtrail Cough" first reported by Dane Wigington of www.geoengineeringwatch.org in 2013, and "Chemtrail Flu," first reported by Alex Jones of www.infowars.com in that same year.

Chemtrail Cough causes respiratory distress and it especially difficult for seniors and children with asthma. Here, you need to be observant of spraying patterns and times. Typically, the first bout of heavy spraying will occur first thing in the morning as the sun rises. Then, during the day, there will be less intensive spraying as the sun crosses the sky. The second heavy bout of spraying will occur as the sun sets. Remember, it takes time for the chemicals to settle; so, as a general rule of thumb, if you must go outside, do it during the afternoon.

However of the three geoengineering spraying concerns, the third is the most disturbing. It is Chemtrail Flu and it is caused by a weaponized pathogenic microplasma produced under a patent held by the Armed Forces Research Institute of Pathology.

If you contract Chemtrail Flu, know that it is not a bacterial or viral infection. Therefore, the drugs used by physicians to treat bacterial or viral infections are ineffective. Victims report the following symptoms:

A general sense of malaise, sinus congestion, sinus drainage, cough, fatigue, body aches, sweating and extreme fatigue. Most report that they do not have enough energy to get out of bed.

While the symptoms vary, persistence is the one constant. The Chemtrail Flu lasts for weeks if not months.

I, myself, contracted Chemtrail Flu on a day where I witnessed especially heavy spraying in the evening towards sunset. It was a cold damp night, and this caused the spraying mixture to cling low to the ground.

The onset was very fast, and by about 3 AM, I was experiencing respiratory distress. Thanks to the advice of natural therapy practitioners, I used a combination of things that bolstered my body's natural immune system. However, what worked best for me was nebulizer therapy. Three times a day I would nebulize using a 50-50 mixture of colloidal silver and distilled water.

Nonetheless, it took me nearly a month to rid myself of it. What is most dispiriting is that you can beat it down and think it's gone, and then it suddenly comes roaring back. When I checked the CDC statistical reporting for colds and flu's during this period of time, what I saw was a man-made statistical cycle. You could see its onset and steady growth of the sickness reports as the spraying program was continued. Then, when the spraying was stopped, the statistical data collapsed.

All I can surmise was our government was monitoring the CDC reports to see the effectiveness and dispersion rates of this weaponized pathogenic microplasma that they were spraying on the populace. A lot of people died unnecessarily in the process, and during the coming tribulation, the spraying of other and more deadly weaponized pathogens should be expected.

Therefore, as a general rule of thumb when doing a relocation site analysis, be sure to explain this to survival community leaders and emphasize that someone should conduct a study of the geoengineering spraying patterns in that area.

Mitigating Volcanic Ash

The last flyby of the Planet X system occurred during Israel's Exodus, and when the 10 plagues of Exodus are reorganized from an allegorical to a scientific order, they snap together like Legos. Of particular concern will be the sixth plague.

In Exodus 9:8 we read, "And the LORD said unto Moses and unto Aaron, Take to you handfuls of ashes of the furnace, and let Moses sprinkle it toward the heaven in the sight of Pharaoh." This is the allegory. The science is that what we're talking about in the sixth plague is volcanic ash resulting from volcanic eruptions. If people breathe it in, it solidifies in their lungs like cement slurry, and they die by suffocation which like drowning is a very unpleasant way to die.

Another problem with volcanic ash is skin boils. Survivors who develop skin boils as a result of unwashed volcanic ash will suffer miserably, and these boils are terribly difficult to treat. Therefore, you must be proactive and make sure that the members of your community have protective clothing. Even if they need to cover themselves with bed linen, anything that will keep the volcanic ash off their bodies is necessary.

For the exposed parts of the body, the ash must be removed. If there is no supply of bathing water, then dig down into the ground for fresh earth or clay and use that to remove the ash. I cannot overstate the importance of doing this as a Survival Wellness Advocate. Remember this.

Solar Radiation Mitigation

When we think of radiation, the first thought that usually comes to mind is radiations from nuclear power plants. This is certain to be a terrible problem during the tribulation as Fukushima type events begin happening worldwide.

In terms of mitigating nuclear radiation there are limited solutions such as Iodine, Nascent iodine, Spirulina, Chlorella, Reishi mushrooms and Magnesium. However, the only effective way to mitigate nuclear radiation is distance. In general you want to be located at least 50 miles upwind of and 100 miles downwind of a nuclear plant. Ergo, distance is the mitigation method. However, with solar radiation, distance takes on a whole different meaning.

During the coming tribulation we're going to experience frequent solar storms. If these storms are Earth directed, and our planet is in the cross-hairs of an event, then that is a problem if you're on the daylight side of the planet.

Solar storms generally come in two stages; there is the flare, and then the coronal mass ejection. The flare is the initial event, and the radiation reaches the surface of our planet at the speed of light, which is approximately eight minutes. The plasma and magnetic fields generated by an Earth directed Coronal mass ejection following the flare can arrive in as little as 14 to 17 hours later.

Consequently, there will be times during the tribulation that going above ground during the day will simply be out of the question. Only at night will members of your community be able to go above ground to forage, scavenge, and tend to other necessary duties.

Here is where distance takes on a new meaning, in that the safe distance between the surface and the top of your head will vary depending on the kind of material that you use.

In Chapter 8 of *Surviving the Planet X Tribulation: A Faith-Based Leadership Guide,* I recommend that for adequate solar radiation protection during the worst of the tribulation, an underground dome shelter should be covered over with ten feet of dirt and two feet of basalt aggregate. However, that is an optimal quick build solution for communities that can afford to do this.

Others will need to work with on hand solutions such as parking garages, train tunnels and so forth. The table below shows different types of materials and the absolute minimum for protection.

Iron, Steel, Volcanic Basalt	4.9" (126 mm)
Brick	14.0" (357 mm)
Concrete	15.4" (392 mm)
Dirt	23.1" (588 mm)
Ice	47.6" (1211 mm)
Soft Wood	61.6" (1568 mm)
Snow	142.1" (3612 mm)

Obviously, the more radiation protection you have overhead the better. Also, members of the community are going to need to be out doing things and they will be exposed to potential solar radiation threats. For this reason, you need to advise community leaders and members about what I call go-to-ground safety zones.

Go-to-Ground Safety Zones

Huddling in bunkers and basements for months and years on end is a sure way to go off the deep end. Rather, life goes on and we take care of families, work at jobs, go shopping, and do all the other normal activities of everyday life. That's why you need to find multiple solar storm survival zones within your everyday travel patterns.

Finding Protection at Home

- Safe rooms
- Storm shelters
- Root cellars
- Basements

Finding Protection in Cities

- Underground parking garages
- Auto and pedestrian tunnels
- Underground subway systems
- Tall buildings with deep basements
- Banks with open vaults
- Catacombs (underground burial crypts)
- Sewage systems
- Storm drain systems

Finding Protection in the Country

- Any cave
- Any mine
- Any tunnel
- Road culverts
- Cliff overhangs
- Natural stone arches

Charged particles from solar flares can begin slamming through your body in just 8 minutes following the eruption, so you need to begin locating these safety zones as soon as possible.

A mantra each member repeats before going above ground is, "Wherever you go, there you are." Looking for these safety zones when you need them is a poor way to plan a tragic death; so start looking for the safety zones in your world today. In time you'll be able to recognize them instinctively, and you can even use your cell phone to help you find less obvious safety zones.

Using Cell Phones to Find Safety Zones

Thanks to modern cellular technology most of us already possess an easy and effective way to find possible safety zones with our cell phones in much the same way Star Trek characters used their trusty little tricorders to find out all sorts of things.

The best way to determine radiation safety zones is with expensive test equipment and the required training to scientifically interpret its results. However, a less precise, but significantly helpful alternative is to monitor the signal strength bars on your cell phone when exploring buildings, caves, tunnels and so forth.

The Rule of Reception: Areas with perfect reception (all bars) should not be considered as solar storm survival zones. Rather, the opposite is true. Areas with good reception are death zones because they do not provide any electromagnetic (EM) shielding!

Always remember that areas located within a cellular footprint and which offer lower levels of reception are likely sources of EM shielding. Obviously, if you're standing in a store in the mall and you're getting five bars of reception on your cell phone, this is not the best place to sit out a solar storm.

On the other hand, the very same mall will usually have a multi-level parking garage. As you walk through the garage, you find a level where your cell phone shows no bars at all. Bingo. That's the place you're looking for.

The bottom line with environmental, radiation and other threats is simple. Just apply the old axiom, "A stitch in time saves nine," with a twist. Instead of a timely effort preventing more work later, it's about being proactive to avoid digging an unnecessary grave in the future.

7

Primary Modalities

Primary modalities are the simple things that you're going to do day in and day out to help community members sustain their own wellness. Call them home remedies if you will, but they work. But do they work better than modern medicine? This question will become moot during the tribulation because there will be no other choice.

Yes, modern medicine offers us amazing things to extend our lives and to ease our pains, but the simple fact is that once the tribulation begins, modern medicine as we know it will have a 3 to 5 day lifespan. After that it will be catch as catch can.

This is because modern hospitals have diesel generators that will continue to provide power to the hospital after the power grid fails. Their fuel bunkers will have enough stored diesel fuel to provide power for 3 to 5 days. Once that gives out and the hospitals go dark, that is when modern medicine ceases to exist as we know it because of its dependency on energy.

America's present healthcare system is very good for the very poor and the very wealthy. Everyone in between, however, is saddled with mind-boggling co-pays and deductibles that reduce insurance coverage to death management policies.

The reason things are as they are is simple to comprehend. America's present medical system is designed to drain the wealth of the middle class into the hands of the elites who own and control the for-profit corporations that operate on the basis of greed as opposed to compassion. Where does this money go? It goes to pay for underground bunkers for the elites who found that healthcare was an ideal way for them to squeeze money out of the populace.

Consequently, Americans who can ill afford this have begun looking for alternatives and this is a good thing. Whether they do it by choice or because of their circumstances, more Americans, than ever before, are treating themselves naturally as a way of preserving what little wealth they have left. This means they are now looking to the past for solutions.

Solutions in the Past

We are now in the information age, before that was the industrial age, and before that the agrarian age.

Looking back, the industrial age began in the coal mines of Great Britain in the mid 18th century. However, the agrarian age began 10,000 years ago. During that time many of the wellness solutions we practice today such as acupuncture, essential oils, yoga, and so forth came into being.

Why do we still use them? That's simple; they work. Furthermore, these agrarian age wellness solutions will also work during a global tribulation and for generations to come. Likewise, so will the best-of-class wellness solutions that came into being during the industrial and information ages.

As a survival wellness advocate, these wellness solutions are the assets in your aid bag and they will come from all three ages: Agrarian, industrial and information. Each will be a time-proven and best-of class-wellness practice. Safe and effective they can all be used in combination without the harmful complications and unforeseen interactions of modern day prescription drugs.

Why have these natural wellness solutions endured for thousands of years? It is for two reasons. First, they cannot be patented. Second, they fall into either of the following categories: They are renewable, a source of knowledge, and readily accessible.

Renewable

Essential oils are an excellent example of wellness solution renewables. All you need are plants and pure water for the source materials and a still or a press to make them.

Knowledge

Self-healing energy arts such as Danjeon Breathing are excellent examples of wellness solution knowledge. Danjeon Breathing dates back to the early days of acupuncture and draws on the same concepts. Developed for Korea's ruling elites, it is quick to learn and easy to do.

It is a good way to deal with the normal aches and complaints of age; however, the driving motive was immune system support. These elites never feared death by starvation or exposure like their subjects, but they were terrified of catching their death of cold. In a tribulation you'll receive the very same healing benefits.

Readily Accessible

Sodium bicarbonate, good old-fashioned baking soda, is a wellness solution that is readily accessible. It is cheap, readily available, and you can buy a 50 pound sack of it for less than a dollar per pound, and it has many health uses.

For example, think about the many brands of toothpaste which feature baking soda as an ingredient. In a survival situation it is not only good for dental hygiene, but more importantly it is a powerful immune system aid for colds, flues, and superbug plagues.

Found in naturally occurring deposits of nahcolit, baking soda is simple to make. However, because you cannot eat it as a food, most will underestimate its value. Barter trade one shotgun shell for a box of baking soda and you're the one coming out ahead on the deal. (And you'll have plenty of takers too.)

Using Primary Modalities

In terms of survival wellness advocacy, the term, primary modalities, refers to the natural remedies and methods you'll employ each day to keep healthy survivors healthy. This term is preferred for a specific reason.

In general, a modality is a particular way in which something is experienced or expressed. However, to a healthcare professional, a modality is the method of application for any therapeutic method or physical agent.

So, when making first contact with a survival community, presenting what you do in terms of primary modalities will help you to define quickly what you do as a survival wellness advocate for the benefit of the community's healthcare professionals.

With that in mind, let's take a look at five modalities. Beginning with the three physical agents, here is the good news; you've already learned something useful about the first one, essential oils.

The important thing to remember about physical agents is the ease with which you can stockpile or find them after modern medicine, as we know it, has come to a screeching halt. This is why I've identified three time-proven, safe, and natural physical agents: Essential oils, colloidal silver, and sodium bicarbonate.

Essential Oils

Your number one physical agent will be the essential oils which I have said previously are a Biblical remedy. If they worked for Moses, they'll work for you. Many of the essential oils are time-tested immune system boosters and offer anti-viral, anti-bacterial, and anti-fungal properties.

As a critical, renewable wellness solution, it is vital that you master the art of essentials oils by learning how to make and apply them. Essential oils are available today in a wide range of prices and qualities. However, for survival purposes though, only one grade will do - Pure therapeutic. To help frame this critical point, let's use brandy for an example.

If you are a connoisseur of fine brandies, you know that Cognac is a brandy; however, all brandies are not a cognac. It is why connoisseurs pay premium prices for brands such as Courvoisier, Hennessy, Martell, and Rémy Martin. These brandies are made from grapes grown exclusively in fields surrounding the town of Cognac, France, twice distilled in copper pots, and aged for at least two years in oak barrels. It is produced under the strict supervision of the French government; there is no brandy better than a Cognac. Everything else is second best.

Similarly, the pure, therapeutic grades of essential oils are like a Cognac. Why use these oils when there are so many bargain basement alternatives out there? Here's why.

Imagine a time during the tribulation; you're hiking along a trail; and you come across a group of strangers huddled by the roadside. As you pass by, you hear them coughing up their lungs. Of course, you pick up the pace to get past them as quickly as possible. But you also know that you have passed through a deadly, viral aerosol haze. Now, what do you do?

With a therapeutic grade essential oil that is safe for internal consumption, as you keep moving down the trail, you put two drops of oil on the tip of your finger, and then rub your finger along the underside of your tongue. This is a sublingual application, and it is the fastest way to get something into your bloodstream. Within a few steps, the antiviral and antibacterial properties in that essential oil will be in your blood stream and boosting your immune system.

On the other hand, let's assume you have a bargain-priced essential oil that is not safe for internal consumption. In that case you get away from the folks coughing up their lungs to a place where you can stop to administer the oil. Now, you sit down, take off your boot, then your sock, and apply the oil to bottom of your foot. (This is the second fastest way to get a substance into your bloodstream.) Afterward, you put your sock and boot back on and on your way you go.

If you are serious about survival, you need to know how to make and use the Cognac of essential oils. With this in mind, let's define the four attributes of a therapeutic grade essential oil that is safe for internal consumption.

- **Non-GMO Source Plant:** What you want are oils made from heritage plant varieties. This means no GMO, because GMO plants are composed of plant and animal genes and those are alien to the human body.

- **Heritage Varieties:** Plants must be sourced from organic farms. This means no use of synthetic agrochemicals or fertilizers, which disrupt the molecular integrity of the plants.

- **Optimal Conditions:** Heritage plant varieties need to be sourced from optimal native growing conditions. This is because plants are plastic in nature; they can adapt to a wide range of soils and climates. However, what you want is a plant grown in an optimal native environment, where it can achieve its full therapeutic potential.

- **Natural Extraction:** How the oils are extracted from the plants is vital. Bargain-priced oils are often extracted with solvents to increase the yields. While they are removed, industrial processes cannot remove 100% of these solvents. Even the smallest amount of solvent residue will render the final oil impure.

Why is it important for you to know these four attributes? Because it is absolutely crucial that you stockpile these seed varieties and learn how to make your own essential oils.

While there is a lot to learn about making essential oils, what you need to know for now, is that there are two basic kinds of extraction, steam distillation and cold press expression.

Making Essential Oils

The most common method used for making essential oils is steam distillation and you can purchase small essential oil distillation stills for making your own oils at home. Just keep in mind that a lot of plant matter is required. For example, it takes 30 lbs of lavender flowers to make 0.5 ounce (15 ml) of therapeutic grade lavender essential oil.

If possible, I strongly urge you to acquire a still and make a few ounces of various oils so you can gain the valuable experience without being under stress. But at the very least, you need to download the schematics from the Internet on how to make an essential oil still.

Then, after you join with a survival community, buddy up with whoever has a hankering to make moonshine whiskey. (There is not much difference between building a still to make moonshine and building one to make therapeutic grade essential oils.)

The other way to make essential oils is called expression. This method is used with plants that are sensitive to the heat required for steam distillation, such as citrus. In this case, a press is used, and like with stills there are models you can purchase for the home.

Again, you'll need a lot of source plants. For example, it takes 45 lemons to make 0.5 ounce (15 ml) of therapeutic grade lemon essential oil.

Stockpiling Therapeutic Essential Oils

In terms of freshness dating, therapeutic grade essential oils are something you can gift your great-grandchildren. When properly made and stored, they can last over a thousand years. In olden times grave robbers would steal valuable essential oils like frankincense first and leave the rest of the booty if they were pinched for time.

Pinched for time is the operative term here because tough times are coming. While we would all love nothing more than to make up vast quantities of our own oils, what we need right now more than anything is to build our range of skills. For this reason, I encourage you to acquire therapeutic grade essential oils, made from heritage plant varieties, and sourced from optimal native growing conditions. This way you can try various oils to see how well they work for you, your family, and your friends.

Now let's move on to our next physical agent, colloidal silver.

Colloidal Silver

Colloidal silver was used extensively by the medical profession as an anti-bacterial prior to the advent of antibiotics in the 1940s. It was used for wound dressings, in creams, and as an anti-bacterial coating on medical devices. After the 1940s, antibiotics were deemed to be more effective.

However, during a tribulation access to modern antibiotics will be extremely difficult if not impossible, and in recent years there has been a proliferation of antibiotic-resistant bacteria.

Even worse, drug companies are more interested in developing more profitable drugs for things like high cholesterol and sexual dysfunction rather than finding alternatives to the antibiotics rendered impotent by these new strains of resistant bacteria.

Today, colloidal silver is readily available as a supplement. People use it for several reasons and report good results. This has resulted in a lot of negative information about colloidal silver. There is a reason for this though; it cannot be patented.

When infections become a leading cause of death, a readily available solution will be better than nothing, and the best thing about colloidal silver is its availability. You can purchase ready-made colloidal silver, or purchase your own device to make it yourself. Not only is colloidal silver good for wound dressings and as a supplement; it's also useful for making potable water.

In fact, electrolytically dissolved silver has been used as a water-disinfecting agent on the Russian Mir orbital space station and the International Space Station because these folks have to drink their own urine; hauling water into space is expensive.

The bottom line with colloidal silver is this: If you show up with a stockpile of ready-made colloidal silver and the knowledge, equipment and materials needed to make it on your own, who is going to turn you away and lose out on a proven antibacterial agent? Next is the third agent. Something you're virtually sure to have in the kitchen.

Sodium Bicarbonate

The third and most commonly available physical agent is sodium bicarbonate, good old-fashioned baking soda. For me, it is the ideal, readily-accessible wellness solution because it is effective for a variety of wellness needs.

Survival in Europe will be easier than in America, because Europe is GMO-free. In America, most folks have stockpiled cheap GMO canned and processed foods, and when all they've got to eat are these alien frankenfoods, their tummies are going to pay for it.

But if you can walk into a survival community with a hundred dollars worth of 10 gr. sodium bicarbonate tablets in your backpack, it's like driving through the front gate in a pickup truck loaded with Alka Seltzer tablets.

Settling upset tummies is great, but that is just the tip of the iceberg when it comes to the many advantages of this readily accessible asset.

In the coming tribulation, the single leading cause of death will be disease, and there is a clear historical precedent. Nick-named the Spanish flu, the Influenza Pandemic, of 1918 was a worldwide horror that reduced the global population by approximately five percent.

The outbreak occurred towards the end of WWI; half of US soldiers who died in Europe fell to this terrible superbug. In America it infected 28% of all Americans. It claimed approximately 675,000 lives and suppressed the average lifespan at that time by 10 years.

However, in New York, a physician by the name of Dr. Volney S. Cheney found an effective way to fight this superbug. He alkalized his patients with baking soda using this simple treatment plan:

- **DAY 1:** Six doses of 0.5 tsp. of Bicarbonate of Soda in glass of cool water, at about two hour intervals.

- **DAY 2:** Four doses of 0.5 tsp. of Bicarbonate of Soda in glass of cool water, at the same intervals.

- **DAY 3:** Two doses of 0.5 tsp. of Bicarbonate of Soda in glass of cool water morning and evening.

- **DAY 4+:** One dose of 0.5 tsp. of Bicarbonate of Soda in glass of cool water each morning until the cold or flu is cured.

Unlike the general population, none of Dr. Cheney's patients died from the Spanish flu, and those who were sick when treated enjoyed full recoveries. In fact, it was so effective the Arm and Hammer Company widely advertised the health benefits of baking soda until the late 1920s until it was forced into silence by competing interests. Yet, there are a wide range of safe uses of this readily accessible asset to include:

- Influenza and Colds
- Dental Hygiene

- Ulcer Pain
- Splinter Removal
- Sunburns
- Deodorant
- Insect Bites
- Foot Soak
- Detox bath with Apple Cider
- Exfoliator Detox bath

Another thing to remember about natural remedies is that unlike prescription pharmaceuticals, they can be used together safely in moderation. For example, you can safely administer baking soda and essential oils together when treating others for superbugs. Plus there is another that you're sure to already have in your medicine cabinet.

Hydrogen Peroxide

Another readily-accessible asset, 3% hydrogen peroxide is a proven antiseptic and disinfectant, and it will likely be found in the medical stores of any community and can be used for colds and flues.

When you come down with a bug, administer a few drops of 3% hydrogen peroxide into each ear. You'll hear some bubbling, which is completely normal, and possibly feel a slight stinging sensation. After 5 to 10 minutes, the bubbling and stinging will subside. After this, drain each ear onto a tissue.

Are there other primary modality physical agents? Of course there are and this is the point of being a member of a Survival Wellness Advocate association or guild. To find, share, and discuss these other readily-accessible physical agents.

Secondary Modalities

Secondary modalities are things that you study on your own, and if you are a member of a survival wellness advocate Guild, you discuss with other SWAs.

However, I want to stress that these are things you need to research. Do not share them with the public at this time, or you may run afoul of agenda-driven sensibilities, special interest financial protectionism and so forth.

Examples of secondary modality physical agents include:

- Alcohol
- Out of Date Prescription Drugs
- Medical Cannabis
- Papaver Somniferum (Opium Poppies)
- Dimethyl sulfoxide (DMSO)
- Miracle Mineral Supplement (MMS)

There may be items on this list you find objectionable, so let's talk about something most people do not find objectionable. FDA approved prescription drugs.

When you research prescription drugs on the Internet, what can you learn? Here are some examples:

- 100,000 Americans die each year from prescription drugs.

- Drug companies pay doctors to be their so-called consultants.

- Doctors are writing prescriptions their financial backers want them to write

- America is the only developed country that doesn't control prescription drug prices.

- Congressman Ron Paul – The *FDA* and Big *Pharma* are "in *bed* together."

The point here is that you must factor in the financial interests of large multinational corporations when reading about any physical agent, if it cannot be patented.

This is because modern medicine has a three-day lifespan. All hospitals have emergency generators and the fuel bunkers for those generators typically contain a three-day supply of diesel fuel. Once the diesel fuel gives out, the hospitals will go dark. At that point, modern medicine will become a catch-as-catch-can proposition.

Obviously, elites will have full access to medicine stockpiles after that, but what about the rest of us? Precious little will be available to us if at all. Therefore, we must prepare to be on our own.

Secondary Modalities — Physical Agents

Although some of these physical agents may offend your sensibilities today, what will you do tomorrow when you have absolutely nothing? Will it be better to say "I trusted naively and was cruelly betrayed, so now I must suffer without hope?" Or do you say, "I knew this was coming and I prepared for the day when something will be better than nothing at all."

This is the reason why you need to study and be aware of these secondary modality physical agents. Many of these have been used as medicines for thousands of years by our forefathers. So here are some practical applications of these physical agents to consider:

- **Alcohol:** If you do not have Vicodin or Oxycondin, alcohol is a reliable pain medicine. Also, in olden times, people would mix water and wine. The alcohol in the wine would kill pathogens in the water and the added water would keep people from getting drunk.

- **Out of Date Prescription Drugs:** As a young Army medic during the mid-70s I was issued medicines, dressings and other physical agents manufactured in the 1940s during WWII. Even though these agents were decades old, they were still safe and effective. So if you have old prescriptions in the cabinet, store them away. You may never need them in the future but a survival community physician may find a good use for them and odds are they'll still be useful.

- **Medical Cannabis:** We often tend to focus on the recreational use of this medicine, but here is a practical use for Cannabis. During a tribulation, your protein sources include such delicacies as rats, grubs, worms and cockroaches. Consequently, a meal will be anything you can keep down without wanting to vomit. If you get the urge to vomit, but need the calories and the food is digestible, smoke a little cannabis and you'll keep it down. It also has a wide range of other survival benefits as well.

There are three principal seed varieties. Indica, sativa and Indica/sativa hybrids. Each has different applications and you may want to stockpile all three. If your State has legalized Medical Cannabis, you can obtain a prescription so you can stockpile medicinal-quality seeds. In states where it has been legalized for recreational use, a prescription is not required.

⬧ **Papaver Somniferum (Opium Poppies):** It legal to purchase these poppies in the USA and to grow them. However, I only recommend stockpiling for now. Also known as BreadSeed Poppies, they contain Morphine, Codeine, Thebaine, and other Alkaloids used by Big Pharma for creating pain medications. Likewise they are used by the Afghans to produce Heroin for criminal distribution. During the tribulation, these poppies can be grown, harvested and processed under the supervision of a physician to create helpful pain medications.

⬧ **Dimethyl sulfoxide (DMSO):** Sold as a solvent and often referred to as horse liniment, this is a powerful anti-inflammatory and some holistic physicians administer it to their patients by IV as an alternative to painful cortisone injections.

⬧ **Miracle Mineral Supplement (MMS):** MMS was originally used in South America as a simple health drink cure for malaria. Discovered in 1996 by an American prospector by the name of Jim Humble it has gained popularity worldwide for a range of ailments such as cancer and arthritis. Banned by law in America and Canada, it is available for purchase elsewhere in the world and physicians in Mexico administer by IV.

There is a lot of information in the form of testimonials by MMS and DMSO users; there is also a lot of disinformation as well. How can you spot it?

Avoiding Special Interest Disinformation

When you search the terms MMS and DMSO, the first page results are typically going to be very negative and will incorpo-rate words such as a scam and hoax. However, there is another term, search engine optimization or SEO for short, you need to know.

Search engine optimization is how you make your message appear on the first page of search engine query results. Special interests make sure their messages dominate the first page results with search engine optimization. An expensive process, which requires continuous and costly professional management, how can you get a more balanced view of things?

Do not read the first results page only. Instead, read through the first five results pages. If you find more positive results pages as you go along, you'll know the first results page is an SEO fabrication paid for by special interests to control the message.

There are other ways to search for honest information as well. Search for videos on YouTube about the agent and look at the thumbs up and thumbs down numbers. If you're not seeing at least a five to one positive ratio, forget it and move on.

Also, read user reviews on Amazon if the products are available for sale. For example, various brands of DMSO and colloidal silver are sold on Amazon.com and typically feature numerous reviews.

The Amazon.com reviews you want to read first are the ones that display "Verified Purchase." These are submitted by customers who actually purchased the product and are far more credible than those submitted by customers with no proof of purchase.

When researching these secondary modalities, you may want to stockpile a few, but at the very least be sure to learn how to make these agents. The formulas and methods are typically on the Internet. Next up are energy healing arts and survivors are going to need them more than you can imagine.

Energy Healing Arts

Often labeled as pseudoscience by the medical profession, many energy healing arts are dismissed by science as unsubstantiated claims, beliefs, or practices that are presented as scientific without the discipline of scientific method. These very same energy healing arts predate modern science as we know it by thousands of years and have endured with great popularity because they are effective.

While scientists are keen to define others, what is needed is a definition for scientists. How about this, "A scientist is someone who says, 'I am the only one with the right to get it wrong, because you're too ignorant to think it through for yourself.'" In other words it is always wise to temper the edicts of scientists with the understanding that they, as humans, are subject to their own ego fallacies also. I say this, as a man who has spent most of his life, as a self-defined born hard geek.

In this chapter rather than debating statistics and protocols, I will share with you my own experiences with energy healing arts and how I see them playing a vital role in survival wellness through the tribulation and beyond. But first, we need to define a suitable energy healing system for the difficult conditions and environments that will need to be endured during the tribulation.

Tribulation Energy Arts

When you explore the popular energy healing arts in practice today, they have ancient roots in nations like China, Korea and Japan. Each has evolved with its own story, but all of the stories are rooted in the need to address afflictions of the body and to bolster the immune system. They functioned in ways that helped people without the reliance on medicinal substances.

During the coming tribulation supplies of the primary and secondary modality physical assets will vary. There will be periods of shortages. The advantage of energy healing arts is that there are no shortages. Energy healing arts draw upon the life force energy of God, as it passes through our bodies, in ways that channel it, unblock it, and intensify it.

There are many different wonderful energy healing arts, but those most suited to the demands of the tribulation will have the following five attributes:

- **Range of Motion Environment:** during the tribulation survivors will spend a great deal of time in confined areas. The practice of an energy healing art must require as little floor space as possible. What I call a range of motion environment where the space that is required is sufficient for the full flexion and extension movement potential of all body joints to be exercised.

- **No Required Specialty Props:** Energy arts often employ exercise props to achieve maximum results for given exercise. As long as those props are optional, or can be easily fabricated with common materials on hand such as blankets, they are acceptable. However, once the use of specialty props is necessary to achieve results, the energy art loses the virtue of portability. In other words, you need to be able to perform an energy healing art in the widest possible number of environments.

◢ **Non-Invasive Techniques:** Acupuncture is an invasive energy art in that practitioners must use needles to channel energy. This requires a necessary supply of invasive instruments, and related treatment assets and tools. If your community is fortunate enough to have an acupuncturist, this person will have been trained through years of study and clinical experience. However, there are noninvasive energy healing arts that offer comparable results which can quickly be mastered for self-help.

◢ **Near Zero Caloric Demands:** Hatha Yoga is one of the greatest ways to keep your body limber and to promote wellness. However, the practice of yoga burns calories. For example a 150 pound woman will burn 189 calories per hour, when doing Hatha Yoga. When food supplies are adequate or plentiful, 189 calories is a pittance to pay for the benefits of this ancient art. However, during the coming tribulation, survivors can expect long periods of near starvation situations where every calorie will be precious. Therefore, energy healing arts with a near zero caloric demand are preferable.

◢ **Effective for Sick Bed Treatment:** All self-healing energy arts offer exercises one can do while in the confines of a sickbed. The question then becomes, are these exercises part of the essential core body of exercises that promote the principal benefits of the art? Therefore a desirable energy art when used in a self-healing application, must offer core benefit exercises for those confined to a sickbed. In situations where the practitioner is applying the art, it must be done in a manner that does not cause additional distress or discomfort for the patient.

One thing that is important to keep in mind is that the energy arts that have been practiced for over a century, must have demonstrated their effectiveness over time. Otherwise, if they were ineffective, they would not have endured. That being said, many energy arts are over a thousand years old. The next time you reach for prescription medicine ask, "Will people be using this medicine 1000 years from now?"

I will now share my personal experiences with two energy healing arts that I believe are ideally suited to the demands and needs of tribulation survivors and also feature the best of the five attributes discussed above.

Japanese Energy Arts

Two ancient and highly effective energy arts that have come out of Japan are Reiki and Jin Shin Jyutsu. Both arts are based on the idea that an unseen life-giving "life force energy" flows through us. When your "life force energy" is low, you are more likely to become sick or stressed. Conversely, when it is high, you tend to experience a happier and healthier general state of wellness.

- **Reiki Therapy:** is often called palm healing or hands-on-body healing because practitioners place their hands lightly on or over a patient's body to facilitate the healing process and reduce stress. You can learn more about this energy art, at www.reiki.org.

- **Jin Shin Jyutsu:** This therapy is another Japanese hands-on-body healing art that balances body, mind and spirit. Jin Shin Jyutsu practitioners use very gentle movements to remove energy channel blockages so energy can move more freely again and to infuse new energy into the body. You can learn more about this energy art, at www.jinshininstitute.com.

Practitioners of both arts use hands-on-body healing techniques to channel energy into the patient. By means of touch they harmonize and energize the body's natural healing processes to restore physical and emotional well-being.

Having received treatments with both methods, I personally have found them to do exactly that. However, of the two the one that had the most impressive results for me was Jin Shin Jyutsu.

In 1999, a massage therapist suggested I take a weekend Jin Shin Jyutsu class and I did. We trained in a hospital like setting. Students would take turns being bedridden patients and then practitioners. In that weekend I learned really valuable techniques that I found simple to learn and effective to employ.

Then in 2000, I was in an auto accident, and I received a serious whiplash injury. I was receiving chiropractic and acupuncture care, which both helped relieve my symptoms. But thankfully for me, my insurance gave me a good deal latitude in selecting my treatments. So, I contacted my Jin Shin Jyutsu instructor from the previous year and began receiving treatments from her.

Compared with chiropractic and acupuncture the treatments were so pleasant and mild that I often fell asleep while she worked on me. However, it was the results that really impressed me. Using my own pain as a measure, I found that noninvasive Jin Shin Jyutsu treatments were equally effective as the invasive acupuncture treatments were for controlling pain. Furthermore, the pain relief I enjoyed from Jin Shin Jyutsu typically lasted over 30% longer than that of acupuncture.

As a survival wellness advocate, learning energy arts such as Reiki, Jin Shin Jyutsu and Reflexology will empower you with highly effective techniques to bring comfort and a sense of wellness to bedridden survival community members. They will love you and those that love them will as well; your presence at their bedside will be welcomed.

However, the one energy art that I believe is the most essential for helping tribulation survivors to overcome health adversities comes from Korea and is called Danjeon Breathing.

Danjeon Breathing

Today, I am a wellness publisher, and the producer and courseware designer for the Feel Better on Your Own Danjeon Breathing for Wellness system (www.feelbetteronyourown.com).

How did I find Danjeon Breathing? The same way others do. You've got a problem and for most it is low back pain. For me it was irritable bowel syndrome. In the summer of 2011, I was encouraged to reduce the red meat in my diet by replacing it with yogurt and other processed food substitutes.

Loaded with corn sweeteners and GMO corn starch as a thickener, it wasn't long before I developed a terrible case of irritable bowel syndrome (IBS). The first thing I learned about modern medicine then was the only thing my family doctor could offer me was an insurance billing code.

It was so bad that it limited the distances I could travel. If I drove more than 25 miles, I would have to overnight in a hotel so that my lower intestine could settle enough for the return home. Having suffered miserably for three months, I turned to Chinese herbal medicines and acupuncture, which tripled my range to seventy five miles. Then in November of that year, I interviewed Roar Sheppard, a Danjeon Breathing Master on my Cut to the Chase program. Afterward he invited me to attend a one-day class he was giving in Berkeley, California in December and I accepted his invitation.

The morning drive to Berkeley was at the extreme range of my IBS endurance and I was a bit pale when I arrived. But Roar and his assistant instructor Paula worked me through the full day of training and I felt immediate and profound relief that day. So much so, I was able to enjoy Thai food (without peanuts) that night instead of my usual IBS diet of bread and potatoes and other such soft foods.

With that I began doing Danjeon Breathing thirty minutes each day, and two weeks later, my symptoms disappeared. Three months later, I knew I had completely resolved my IBS issue because I could begin eating peanuts again. Trust me, if you have IBS and eat peanuts, it will leave you begging for a merciful death.

As a former courseware developer in the Silicon Valley and a Planet X researcher and author, I knew then why God had led me down this particular path. While there are many wonderful energy arts, Danjeon Breathing is the ideal energy art for tribulation survival. This insight led me to develop and produce the Feel Better on Your Own Danjeon Breathing system.

The first goal was to create an inexpensive, self-paced, home study course for men and women from the age of forty-five to sixty-five. The second was to develop courseware that would be intuitive to Western minds with a rapid access to knowledge design.

Medic Aid Bag Design

At the outset I began studying other materials on the art, and like most Eastern instruction, it can be a bit obtuse for Western thinkers. Therefore, I asked myself, "What would be the best way to explain this Eastern self-healing energy art to Western thinkers?"

The answer took me back to my late teens when I became an Army medic with a 91 Bravo rating. At that time the rating was equivalent to a licensed practical nurse, and what I learned stayed with me over the decades and became the template I used to design this program.

When you design a training system like this, you must first visualize the finished product. What I visualized was the aid bag I carried as a young medic.

It was the perfect model for this system. Because I knew where everything was in my aid bag, I could get at it quickly. Consequently, the Feel Better on Your Own Danjeon Breathing for Wellness system is in my mind no different than the aid bag I carried as an Army medic. Sure, I couldn't do everything with it; I could do what mattered most.

These experiences redefined my wellness journey and set me on a course of discovery. The realization was if we are to survive the tribulation, we need to look to the past for solutions for the future.

Catching Your Death of Cold

Danjeon Breathing was created by wealthy and powerful Korean elites during the early days of acupuncture for longevity, relief from aches and complaints, and to bolster the immune system.

The ruling elites of ancient Korea did not fear starvation, exposure, and the other threats which plagued their subjects. In addition to assassination their greatest fear was "catching their death of cold" as the old saying goes.

It was this very fear that propelled the methodical refinement of the most essential Danjeon Breathing exercises over the centuries. Their health and wellness concerns were about finding a simple way to deal with the normal aches and complaints of age and to boost their immune systems.

Impressed with the results the Chinese were enjoying with acupuncture, they searched for a simpler way to obtain the benefits of acupuncture without invasive needles and a continuous dependency on schooled practitioners.

This is why these ancient Korean elites funded the development of Danjeon Breathing. They got more than they had hoped for. They got a simple way to store life force energy in the region of the body where seventy percent of the human immune system resides.

Danjeon Breathing Boosts Your Immune System

The practice of Danjeon Breathing method is centered on the lowest region of the body cavity. This is why the first thing you do is center your focus on an area of the body women call the womb; it resides above the pelvic girdle near the base of the spine. Koreans describe this region as the Danjeon. This focus yields three powerful immune system benefits:

- Opening of energy channels throughout the body and clearing blockages.

◢ Focused breathing substantially increases the level of oxygenation in your blood.

◢ Fueling a slow release of added life force energy in the body stored in the Danjeon.

Like Reiki and Jin Shin Jyutsu, Danjeon Breathing uses the life energy that surrounds us and which is in the air and water and is also known as Chi (from Chinese), Ki (Japanese) or Prana (Indian.)

All you need is an area large enough to give you a range of motion environment and no special props are required. This non-invasive energy art is simple to learn and features gentle, near zero caloric demand exercises that are beneficial in terms of general muscle tone and elasticity.

Immune System Support in Twenty Minutes a Day

The intended goal of all Danjeon Breathing poses is to open energy channels throughout the body. This way the flow of life force energy and oxygen throughout the body can be optimized through movement, focus and visualization with each pose.

After centering your focus on your Danjeon, you inhale and visualize Life force energy entering through the top of your head and passing down through your body to your Danjeon.

On exhale, you visualize yourself expelling the residual spent life force energies in your Danjeon out and down through your legs and then out through your feet.

After a few days of doing the exercises, you'll become attuned to the energy sensations. Most practitioners know they've recharged their Danjeon when they feel what is often called a pleasant, "Peppermint Patty" sensation on the balls of the feet.

In terms of future tribulation survivors, how fortunate it is that this wonderful energy healing art was funded by Korean elites who demanded a KISS solution, "Keep it simple stupid."

But here is another wonderful benefit. Danjeon Breathing can also give you "survival kung fu" as I call it. So, what is that?

Assume that a tsunami is coming your way. With survival kung fu you'll realize it several seconds before anyone else around you does. What advantage can that give you?

As that wall of water races up the street, you'll already be on the second or third floor of the building while everyone else is scrambling at the base of the stairs. That's survival kung fu and you automatically develop it after about three to six months of doing your breathing for 20 minutes each day. To learn more about Danjeon Breathing, visit www.feelbetteronyourown.com.

10

Related Advocacy Skills

When I talk with the newly aware about prepping for the tribulation I often have this mental image in my mind of them racing up and down the aisles, pushing a loaded cart with wobbly wheels through a big box store screaming, "Oh my God, they're out of Tabasco sauce. We're all going to die!"

While there is no question about the need for bullets, beans, and bunkers, what is most important is not the having the things. Rather, it is the knowing of things, and this is the reason why you need to build as robust a set of related advocacy skills as possible.

To illustrate the point let's look at some additional advocacy skills to help you establish your value as a member of a future survival community.

Survival Water Sourcing and Purification

Water is life. Having clean potable water to drink and reliable sources for it and for its other uses are a fundamental necessity. It can be a little difficult to find classes about survival water sourcing and purification.

However there are some excellent books you can use and in chapter 7 of '*Surviving the Planet X Tribulation*', I recommend the following: '*The Rainwater Harvesting*' series of books by Brad Lancaster.

Drought will be a real problem in many areas during the tribulation and this man has written books that help you to find sources of water in dry climates. While Brad's books are sizable and take time to read, the '*The Preppers Water Survival Guide*' by Daisy Luther is a small book you can stuff in your back pocket that will give you a huge advantage during the tribulation. Daisy explains how to get water cleaned, and how to go about determining if a well offers truly potable water.

Hygiene and Sanitation

There is a problem that men see far more often than women when it comes to using public toilets, secret poopers. These are people who get some perverted, vicarious thrill from not flushing a public toilet so that others have to see the majesty of their creation. Ugh, what disgusting human beings these people are.

Today, all we can really do is flush the toilet and get on with life. During the tribulation these people are going to become incredibly dangerous. Communities can spend large sums of money to build sophisticated shelters that can withstand natural and man-made threats. Yet, all it will take is one secret pooper to go to the bathroom, and then straight to work in a common kitchen area without any sense of responsibility for personal hygiene. This is when all it takes is one small fleck of fecal matter to get into a community meal and the next thing you know, people are dying left and right of some horrible communicable disease like Cholera.

Here is where your tax dollars have done some excellent work for you. As a former Army medic, I strongly urge you to purchase or download excellent books on field hygiene and sanitation such as the Army Field Manual FM 21-10 (Field Hygiene and Sanitation). You can buy a print edition online; there are also freely available PDF versions that you can download as well. Plus, there are web sites authored by kind and knowledgeable people. Search for them and save useful pages to your computer for future reference.

First Aid Training

If you're not already trained, I strongly urge you to take a Red Cross Adult and Pediatric First Aid/CPR/AED course. When you've been certified in this course, a community physician will see you as having a valuable skill. They will know that you have been competently trained how to deal with typical first aid emergencies such as burns, cuts, scrapes, and back injuries.

You will have also been trained how to deal with heart attacks. You will learn CPR, which stands for cardiopulmonary resuscitation, and AED, the use of an automated external defibrillator. Community physicians are always interested in finding an extra pair of hands, and this basic training will make you a more valuable asset.

Reflexology

Something that is easy to learn on your own is reflexology. You can download free reflexology image maps of the feet from the Internet. There are also a number of well-written books available online for purchase.

When people are sick and experiencing pain, this simple practice offers a gentle way to bring relief. Best yet, finding volunteer test subjects is as easy as making microwave popcorn.

Hospice and Palliative Care Giving

Another skill set you can add is a certification as a volunteer hospice or palliative caregiver. The need for this skill set will be great during a tribulation when there will be a tremendous amount of death and dying.

Volunteer caregiver courses can give you critical skills community physicians and leaders will understand and appreciate, such as:

- Companionship for patients and families
- Simple care giving tasks for patients
- Providing bereavement support for families

My guess is that you might have a few ideas running around in the back of your mind about things you have developed on your own that might be suitable as a related advocacy skill. If so, you're already demonstrating what will be one of your most valuable skills as a survival wellness advocate, resourcefulness.

Self-Assessment

In this chapter we have only discussed a handful of additional skills to help you become more valuable to a survival community. Enough, I hope to get the gears in your head turning. If you are in awareness, you will undoubtedly have had a life filled with interesting adventures where you learned things and acquired skills for reasons other than having something to say on a job resume.

Whether they were a part of your wellness journey of discovery or a burr under your saddle, you have picked them up along the way. As a survival wellness advocate, you need to reflect back on those experiences with a thoughtful self-assessment. You just might be surprised at how versatile you already are.

Knowledge Mountain Guilds

Up to now everything you have learned about Survival Wellness Advocacy can be applied on a local level, whether with your own family and friends or within a larger survival community. But for those of you who are interested in the BIG WIN as explained previously, humanity is not going to have a Star Trek future unless we pull together to make it happen.

Conversely, those who pursue "me and mine survival strategies" will live in fear of discovery by ruthless predators and this will certainly happen. I call these people "bunker bunnies." Even though they may be armed with expensive weapons, predators will stalk them and strike at an inopportune moment, inflicting death and terrible suffering.

This is why strength in numbers is the core strategy of my book, *Surviving the Planet X Tribulation,* where I emphasize the need to create spiritual communities of 100 or more survivors. If these same communities want to enhance their survivability and make a difference in the post tribulation future, even greater things are possible. To accomplish this, they need to join with similar communities, and it will require the ability to work within a trusted communication network.

This is one of the principal reasons why I founded the Knowledge Mountain Church of Perpetual Genesis in 2015. The church will not only be in service to God's mission of perpetual Genesis through service to others; it will also create a communication solution so isolated communities can connect with each other. This mission is also based on the church's three precepts of self-sufficiency knowledge, hope for the future, and knowing that you are not alone.

If your curiosity is piqued enough that you have an interest in possibly joining such an effort, then you should become a member of the church. Now, let's see what that entails.

About Knowledge Mountain Church

We are an online teaching church that teaches universal truths and do not offer ourselves as a replacement faith. As the old saying goes, "If it ain't broke, then don't fix it." Ergo, our role is not to replace other faiths, but to fill in the gaps for those in awareness, with tribulation survival needs that transcend the limited teachings, dogma, and doctrine of their present faiths.

Our mission is to be in service to others by helping them to survive the coming tribulation with self-sufficiency knowledge. It is also to help usher in an age of Enlightenment for all of humankind with messages of hope for the future and the knowledge that you are not alone.

If this mission appeals to you and you wish to join with us, you must embrace our mission, provided your core faith allows you to venture beyond its paradigm.

Is this your cup of tea?

If your present faith forbids entertaining outside doctrine and dogma, then you should restrict your interest to providing for those who share the same limited worldview. If this is the case, the remainder of this chapter will be of no interest to you. Please skip ahead to the next chapter.

On the other hand, if you think this could be your cup of tea, then please, read on.

Tribulation Communications

Within the first two years of the coming tribulation, 90% of the telecommunications infrastructure required to operate the Internet will probably be destroyed or disabled. At this point the Internet as we presently know it will cease to exist. What will remain will be piecemeal local solutions and possibly some fragments of the military's and government's communication systems which of course will be unavailable to the general populace.

The collapse of the rule of law and the government along with degraded atmospheric conditions will largely disrupt our ability to conduct long-haul communications outside of local areas. Consequently, communication will be reduced to local CB traffic and HAM station-to-station radio traffic in the VHF and UHF bands.

As atmospheric conditions improve over time, HAM radio operators will be able to resume long-haul HF communications to stations outside of their local areas.

Meanwhile, the Internet will need a decade or more to be reestablished to a shadow of its present self. But before then, what emerges is what I call an AlterNet which will be based on mesh network technology.

What is a mesh network? Instead of using an Internet provider like Comcast or AT&T to send information to others, your computer will relay other computer messages in the background. In a sense, each user's computer will also serve as a relay station for an ad-hock AlterNet.

Yes, this is geeky, and yes, you cannot run down to the store today and buy a mesh network modem. So, how on the earth is a mesh network alternative going to come into being without the necessary technology? Who says we do not have it? I didn't.

We Already Have AlterNet Technology

Today, millions of readily accessible devices are already installed throughout our towns and cities and talented people will quickly learn how to adapt them for use in a mesh network alternative. These devices are called Smart Meters. The elites presently use them to monitor our home and business energy usage. Ostensibly, it is supposed to create a more balanced and energy-efficient power grid which is nonsense.

The whole purpose for Smart Meters is to spy on us. Elites can use them to monitor our daily activities. With the information these gadgets provide, they can learn when we get up in the morning, when our children come home from school, when the family sits down to dinner, and so forth. This may seem pointless now, but wait until Marshal Law is declared and folks begin to realize that they've been setup to fail. Then the elites will begin using real time Smart Meter data feeds to determine an optimal time for Homeland Security forces to smash front doors and make arrests.

However, once the power grid fails, these Smart Meters will be useless to the elites and a surprise gift for the rest of us. They can then become the enabling technology of an AlterNet, and there are two reasons for this. First, Smart Meters already use a form of mesh networking and second, they are designed for use with a power grid and are therefore highly survivable against EMP radiation.

Who'll make this work? In my book, *Surviving the Planet X Tribulation*, I explain that the leaders of faith-based survival communities always need to encourage the "3 I's" of invention, insight, and initiative. All they need to do is find people with the talent, skills, and the knowing of things and inspire them to become AlterNet Energizer Bunnies. They will and it will work. You may shake your head but not me. I believe in people and what they can do when they are properly motivated.

The question becomes, how will our church participate in this noble cause? I have a plan.

Connecting Survivors

To imagine this plan, think back to when you set up your Internet connection in the house. In the back of the modem that your Internet Service Provider (ISP) gave you, were different cable connections. One was for the phone jack or the cable TV cable and another to your computer. Or perhaps, there was one to a home router that allowed you to connect multiple computers to your modem via high-speed cables or Wi-Fi.

The wire that you plugged into the modem that connects it to your Internet service provider is easily recognized because it has three letters next to it, "WAN" which stands for wide area network. A wide area network is how you connect your computer and all of your other devices in your home to the World Wide Web.

Now, what about the other plug in the back of the modem? You use it to connect your computer or home router to the modem. It is easily recognized because it has three letters next to it "LAN" which stands for local area network.

The plan is for Knowledge Mountain Church of Perpetual Genesis to create Open Source Guilds with an enterprise model based on these simple WAN/LAN concepts.

If you're wondering what open source means, it is the opposite of proprietary. Proprietary refers to having the characteristics of ownership or being privately owned; having a patent or using with an exclusive legal right.

People who develop and freely share software and content do so with an open source approach. All that they ask is to be recognized for their contributions which is really fair. To facilitate this open source way to share knowledge with other survivors, our church offers an enterprise model which is based on open source guilds.

Open Source Guilds

Why did our church create an enterprise model based on open source guilds since the term "guild" is seldom in use these days? There is a specific reason.

A Guild is an association of people for mutual aid or the pursuit of a common goal. The term dates back to medieval times when groups of craftsmen and merchants formed guilds to establish best practices and standards and in some cases to limit competition.

Today, we see guilds serving more modern roles with different names, such as: associations, societies, unions, leagues, cooperatives, fellowships, clubs, orders and lodges to name a few.

Once our governments and law and order collapse during the tribulation, survivors will live through a transition period that will be akin to medieval times, but with a difference. In this future, honorable guilds can serve an instrumental role in providing a clean slate for the beginning of the next civilization. This will be a time when we will honor the person, the land, and the community as part of a larger ecosystem of hope for the future. With this in mind, we created two church guilds based on the WAN/LAN model.

Survival Wellness Advocacy Guild (LAN)

As a Survival Wellness Advocate, you communicate on a local basis within the community you serve. In other words, you are part of a local area network (LAN). In your role as a Survival Wellness Advocate, you are a member of a community and it goes no further.

However, as a member of the Knowledge Mountain Church of Perpetual Genesis Survival Wellness Guild, you acquire WAN access through our The Radio Free Earth Guild, which is a part of an autonomous enterprise operated by Knowledge Mountain Church members for long-haul communications.

The Radio Free Earth Guild (WAN)

The purpose of our Radio Free Earth Guild will be to fill the vacuum left behind when currently established governing authorities like the (Federal Communications Commission (FCC) and independent governing bodies like the *American Radio Relay League (ARRL)* cease to exist.

This Guild will create an open source standard for objectives and qualification procedures in order to create trusted human networks of HAM radio operators that will help communities communicate over long distances with each other.

It will also provide self-sufficiency programming content for survivors that will be both informative and entertaining. This programming harkens back to the 1930s when radio helped Americans pulled through the hardships of the Great Depression. Then, Americans could laugh and forget their troubles when they heard Amos and Andy making jokes about their Stutz Bearcat motorcar.

During the tribulation, this format will be employed with the difference. There will be a new Amos and Andy, but his time instead of making jokes about their Stutz Bearcat, they'll be making jokes about solar cells, water pumps and so forth and how to fix them.

Likewise, there will be the soap operas, and these too will serve an informative role. For example a daytime soap opera about midwives will have the usual human dramas to sigh about. However, the listeners will also hear along the way useful information about necessary things like prenatal care and how to manage difficult deliveries.

Where will this information come from? Much of it will come from subject matter experts and Survival Wellness Advocate Guild members.

Want to Know More?

To learn more about the Knowledge Mountain Open Source Guilds and to join with others to make a difference, please visit our web site at www.knowledgemountain.org.

Part 3 – Righteous Voices

Scenario

We will see governments collapse during the tribulation along with law and order as we know it today. Consequently, survival communities and groups are going to have to manage on their own without public safety nets. In this environment they are certain to run afoul of modern sensibilities.

For example, when I'm confronted by a woman who believes in strict gun legislation, refuses to arm herself, and then takes great umbrage with the need for self-defense, I always respond with the same question, "How many times do you need to be raped before you pick up a gun?" This inevitably ends the conversation with a glaring silence. The point here is that we are going to live in a tough world during the tribulation where death will be persistently lurking in the shadows.

As a Survival Wellness Advocate, you will be needed to help community members adjust to this new reality which will largely eviscerate their sensibilities. Likewise, you will also be needed to help community leaders make impossible decisions and not just once in a while, they'll happen every day.

I have prepared the following scenario with this in mind. It takes place two years into the tribulation and the setting is in a rock mine that has been converted into an underground shelter. The community of approximately 100 people does the best it can to replace rotted shoring timbers and to address safety issues on an ongoing basis. However, earthquakes are problematic, and unsupported ceilings are subject to crumbling and cave-ins. Yet, if the community relocates above ground, it faces certain death for at least another year.

The scenario begins in the small two-room compartment of Janet Konow, a recent widow with two little children. It is late afternoon, and the children are at school.

Day 1 – Afternoon

Charlie Cantrell set down his toolbox next to a water station and leaned his five foot long, pointed steel bar and step ladder against the wall. He then pulled out the small, grimy notebook he carried in his back pocket. It was the last work order of the day, and it had been a long day for a tired man. His scribbled note read, "Drift three, compartment two. J. Konow. Rock damage." Charlie soaked a clean rag in the basin and wiped the grime off his face, then lingered for a few minutes to catch his strength.

Janet was making tea when Charlie knocked on the corrugated tin used to partition the compartments. She pulled aside the curtain that served as her front door to see a tired man in his late 30s. Tall and lanky, his unkempt long brown hair was already streaked with occasional signs of gray, and the bags under his eyes were large enough to carry luggage.

"You've got rock fall damage?" Charlie asked.

"Yes. It happened yesterday during the small trembler. Some heavy stones fell from the ceiling onto the corner of the back room where my children sleep. Nothing big, it just dented ceiling. So, I thought it was best to report it. Lucky for you, the kids are in school, so they won't be underfoot."

"Ah heck, I like rug rats," Charlie replied with a smile. "No problem for me. Okay, let's take a look at it."

Janet stepped aside to let him in, and Charlie walked to the back room. In the far corner he could see that the bracing for the corrugated tin ceiling had been damaged. It was a typical problem in the old mine and one that could be quickly fixed. Setting up his stepladder he inspected the damaged brace and removed it for repair.

As he was stepping back down, Charlie lost his balance, and the damaged brace flew out of his hand nearly striking Janet in the face as he fell to the ground. Sprawled on the floor, he moaned and shook his head, "Damn clumsy of me."

Janet knelt beside him and put a hand on his shoulder. "You okay?" Embarrassed, he nodded yes, and she sighed with relief. "Charlie put this aside for a minute and come with me. I just made tea, and it's Earl Grey."

Getting up from the floor Charlie asked, "Earl Grey? Where on earth did you find that?"

"A barter trade," she said. "Come on." Janet led him to the front room where a small table was mounted to a corner with two small benches. They slide onto the benches, and as Janet lifted the cozy from her teapot she asked, "Why are you so tired Charlie?"

"Problems with the wife," he answered reluctantly.

Janet rubbed her chin remembering he married a recent newcomer to the community a few months ago. "I remember now; your wife is that new dental hygienist. She's the one who came with all of her instruments. How come you're not sleeping? Are the two of you are trying to make a baby?"

"No, I'm living in a nightmare with a woman who thinks I'm a monster."

"Whoa, as I recall, you were just married a few months ago. What happened? Why is the honeymoon over?"

Charlie glanced away; Janet reached and gently took hold of his arm. "You can tell me Charlie because whatever you say doesn't go beyond this room. It's just that you look like you need to talk to somebody about it; you can talk to me."

He rubbed his furrowed brow, and his hands were covering the sad gaze of his blue-gray eyes. "Desiree and I courted for six months; it was wonderful; and the first three months after the marriage were equally amazing. Just when I thought, I'm a lucky guy; it happened."

"What happened Charlie?"

"One day, when we were alone by ourselves, suddenly out of nowhere she's starts screaming hysterically, pulling her hair, throwing things and going on about old memories she couldn't stop coming back into her mind. It was terrifying. I never saw her like this before. I didn't know what to do; so, I was just quiet until she settled down. I guess I was kinda in shock."

"And then what happened?"

"That's when I learned for the first time that these memories haunted her. She was 13 years old when she was gang-raped by three neighborhood boys from influential families. After she had told her father, he put a lid on it and did nothing. All I can figure is that one or more these other families had some dirt on him, so he abandoned his daughter to save his own skin."

The revelation made Janet wince, but she maintained eye contact with Charlie because experience had taught her there would be more. This tortured man was finally able to unburden his soul with a stranger.

Charlie continued, "Then she told me when she was a teenager, she went to live in New Orleans and started running with a pretty radical group of kids down in the French Quarter. She told me she had become a totally rebellious young girl. That was okay I suppose, but what hurt was she said that she was date raped multiple times. It appears that the boys she ran with all knew that they could get her drunk, then date rape her, and she would do nothing about it. So, they passed her from one to the other, all having their fun with no expense."

With that, his head sagged as his eyes began to well up with tears. "Then she told me that she became an angry woman and slept with more men than she could remember. She said that she would just call men she hardly knew and invite them over to her place for sex and they would always come. After years of that, she said she finally grew out of that phase of anger when she got religion."

Janet poured the tea as the last of his words sank in. She had heard plenty of abuse stories similar to this. Before the tribulation, she and her husband had been foster parents and it was time to go beyond what to the why. "Go on Charlie; tell me how you felt about all this beginning with that first day when Desiree revealed all this to you?"

Charlie enjoyed a slow sip of the tea and smiled at her appreciatively. It had been a long time since he had a real cup of tea. "This is excellent tea and thanks for sharing it with me." Janet just smiled. "Well, after the shock, I felt like I was going to a funeral. To learn about all this three months after we were married stung. It was like the woman I courted, fell in love with, and married had just died. The angry woman now sharing my bed was someone I wouldn't care to know."

Janet placed her hand on top of Charlie's, "Why is that?"

Charlie stared bleakly at the table for a moment before answering. "To be honest, I felt betrayed. I stood before the altar with her and took my vows with love and honorable intentions. I deserved to know these things before I did that. Learning it all after only three months, I felt kinda like learning after the honeymoon that your wife committed adultery on your wedding day." He rolled his head back and forth, then added, "Well not really adultery, but damned if it didn't hurt just as bad."

"But there's more isn't there Charlie? How you feel about it?"

He closed his eyes and took a deep breath. "God this is an awful thing to think let alone say."

"Say it."

"All of this left me feeling like I was the last guy in a long line of men who had been with her. It's like being the last one to show up to a dinner party, and the first thing that happens when you walk through the door is someone hands you the check. But that wasn't the worst of it."

She sensed what was coming next but knew Charlie needed to find his words. "Like I said Charlie, this is just between you and me; nobody else will ever know."

He gazed into her eyes thankfully, "She's using me as a human punching bag now. She's 'tarring me with an old brush,' as they say and punishing me for what all those men did, and it's making my life hell. Nobody in my life has ever made me feel as dirty and as filthy as Desiree has, and it's tearing me up inside."

"And you feel like you're walking on eggshells?"

"No, it's worse than that. I feel like I'm walking barefoot on broken glass because I don't know what will set her off again. Now we use code words for things that I could talk about like the word sex. If I mentioned that word in any context, she'd go crazy on me. Now we have a code word for sex, cuddling."

Janet nodded her head appreciatively, "And now you live in fear of forgetting to use the right code words and inadvertently creating another crisis?"

"That about gets it. I'm living in fear. I don't sleep well and sometimes I just can't eat I'm so upset."

Charlie's loss of appetite was a red flag for Janet. "Whoa Charlie, we barely get enough calories each day to keep going as it is and you're so upset that you sometimes cannot eat. I'm very sorry to hear this because I have seen it before. The shrinks call it transference, and it sounds like Desiree is acting out her suppressed rage towards her abusers, and you're the target. I've seen how hurtful this can be."

"That's an understatement."

"So have you discussed this with anyone else like your family, or even better one of the Survival Wellness Advocates? You know you can talk to them in confidence about things like this."

He shook his head, "My mom and I talked about it, and she says we have to deal with it on our own. We should also keep it from my twin sister, Judy since she's six months along. Mom is afraid that if Judy learns what's happening with Desiree and me, it could complicate the pregnancy."

Janet nodded her head appreciatively. "Yes, keeping Judy out of the loop is probably for the best, but I still think you should talk with an advocate. Given you've only been married for a few months, I'm sure one of the advocates would be able to help."

Charlie shrugged his shoulders. "But they're all women; if I talk to them, they'll just circle the wagons around Desiree, and I'll look like a monster."

Janet shook her head. "Charlie, you should give the advocates more credit than that. They're good women; they'll respect your feelings and want to help you and Desiree."

"No!" he answered firmly. "Mom and I talked a lot about it, and it comes to the same thing. Desiree said she explained her abuse history during her induction interviews. Mom is afraid that if we say anything, even to an advocate, they'll want to defend a bad call by making me look like the bad guy. You know how it is. Once an innocent man is accused of being an abuser, he's forever painted as a testosterone-driven monster. I'm between a rock and a hard place and I don't see a way out."

Janet swallowed the last of her tea and set her cup down. "I see your point, Charlie. I can also see that you are angry and feeling betrayed. The only thing I can think to say is that you need to rise above your own feelings so that you can help Desiree overcome this crisis. It's a shame you feel like you cannot talk to an advocate. I do not believe your mother's fears are justified, though as a mother, I can see her concerns. Please reconsider."

Charlie looked at her stoically for a few moments and slid out of his bench and stood up. "Okay, I'll think about it, and maybe hash it over with mom again. But she's mighty afraid that an advocate will tell me I'm a cruel and unsympathetic husband. I guess I'm just going to have to tough this out until something happens to change things. In meanwhile though, I need to fix that corner brace so we can keep the rocks off your kid's heads."

"Just a simple repair," Janet replied.

"It will only take a few minutes, and I'll be on my way. I do dozens of these repairs each week. It just comes with sheltering in an old mine. I'll be finished real quick and out of your hair."

"No need to rush Charlie. Like my father used to say, 'Measure twice; cut once.'"

He smiled, "He must have been a carpenter." Janet winked in acknowledgment. "I'll just get to it and be on my way. Thanks again for talking with me today. Talking with my mom hurts because she hates Desiree for causing me all this pain."

"You're a good man, Charlie, and your mother is a good woman, but she's perhaps a bit overprotective. Again, I strongly urge you to see an advocate. It will be a step in the right direction in getting out from between this awful rock and the hard place you see yourself in."

"OK, Janet. I'll think on it and thanks again. Talking with you has really helped. In fact, it's the first time anything really has helped, and thank you for keeping it our secret."

Day 4 – Pre-Dawn

Janet woke late in the night and trundled off to the makeshift toilets near the entrance of the drift to relieve herself. Aside from the slight smell of methane, the compost toilets worked reliably well.

Alice, her neighbor, had just finished her toilet and stepped out to find Janet waiting for her. "I would sell my soul for a good French bidet," Alice joked.

Janet laughed, "Who knows maybe someone might..." She froze mid-sentence as both women felt the ground tremble beneath. They looked into each other's eyes with an instant knowing: Earthquake and not a small trembler like before.

First the roar, then it hit like a freight train as both women took cover. Then they heard the sickening sound of a cave-in as parts of the unsupported ceiling in the drift collapsed.

Mortified, they waited for the quake to settle and quickly ran back to their compartments. Alice was the first to reach hers, and she found her husband safely curled up in a corner. It was then that Janet's screams echoed off the drift walls of the mine. "Oh my God, my babies, my babies! Help me, please, somebody help me."

Alice's husband looked at her with sad alarm. No words were needed. He bolted upright and began gathering his safety gear. "Get the lanterns, Alice," was all he could say as Janet's hysterical screams continued to pierce the darkness again, and again.

Day 4 – Noontime

The last to arrive was the community leader, Johnathon Brown. He arrived to the Council chambers with a heavy heart. Seated around the circular table were Jordan Campbell, Shelter Engineer, Fante Adebo of Human Services, Patrica Heally, Security Chief and also representing Dr. Barbara Moss of the Medical Services group, and Advocate, Alicia Townsend.

Johnathon sat down and gazed into their eyes and then began "Since we are still in the midst of this crisis, what I need from each of you is a quick assessment of where things stand before we go to an open discussion. Starting with you Jordan, where are we with drift three?"

"That cave-in was a bloody mess for sure," Jordan began. "It's still too hard to tell if three of them can be saved, but all of the rest have minor damage. There's nothing immediate there, but mind you, we were damn lucky the quake didn't last another four or five seconds. If it had, we'd have lost a fourth of our population." The revelation stunned everyone in the room, as shocked glances flipped back and forth.

"Fante," Johnathon said. "What about the affected families in three?"

"We've cleared everyone out of the drift and relocated them to other compartments. Folks are doubling up and happy to help out. No complaints, though we could use more compost toilets in a few areas."

"Give me a day Fante," Jordan replied, "and I'll have it done. Just tell me where you need them."

Fante nodded thankfully. "Will do, I'll get a work order to you this evening."

Johnathon shifted his gaze towards his security chief. As a tough-minded assistant police chief before the tribulation, Patrica was the kind of person who always seemed to get a clear bead before others could get their heads around a situation. "I know that look on your face Patrica; it doesn't look good."

"Sir, we've got more rumors flying around here than buzzards over a dead Buffalo. People are starting to get angry that we lost two beautiful children because Desiree Cantrell is racing around and telling anybody who will sit long enough to listen to her that it's all Charlie's fault. Her husband is responsible for these deaths because he is an abusive husband who only thinks about himself. I'm worried that things could get ugly here if we don't get a quick handle on the situation."

"Jordan," Johnathon interrupted, "isn't Charlie Cantrell in your group?"

"Yes."

"So is there anything to this? Is Charlie at fault here?"

Jordan squirmed in his chair as all eyes in the room focused on him. "Well, yes and no."

"What kind of bullshit answer is that?" Fante shot back.

Her retort earned an angry glance from Jordan. "Charlie was the last one to do a repair in three, about three days ago. The problem was in the back room of Konow's two room compartment where her kids were sleeping when the quake hit."

"So, was Charlie's repair faulty?" Johnathon asked.

"That's impossible to say," Jordan answered matter-of-factly, "but what I can tell you is this. Those kids did not need to die. We have a standard safety inspection procedure any time we do rock fall repairs and Charlie Cantrell failed to do it. Had he performed a safety check, we would have temporarily relocated the families in there while we made the necessary repairs. It breaks my heart to say this, but if Charlie had followed procedure, those two beautiful kids would still be alive today."

Patrica Heally, as did everyone else in the room, immediately perceived Charlie's culpability, but she was the first to voice it. "Why didn't Charlie perform a customary and usual safety check when the circumstances required it?"

Rubbing his chin, Jordan scanned the room for moral support and could find none. "It was the first question I asked, so it's fair. For the record, I asked Charlie the same question before Doc had him strapped to a gurney and sedated. Look folks, he's on suicide watch right now; so can we all at least attempt to be a wee bit understanding?"

Patrica was about to speak up when Johnathon motioned to her to refrain. "Jordan, we're all trying to come to grips with this. The last thing any of us needs to do is to make the situation any worse than it already is. So please, share with us Charlie's explanation."

"He was screaming and beating on himself when I talked to him and he just kept saying that he forgot and begged God to forgive him. Then the Doc doped him. At this point, when he's conscious, he doesn't even know his own name. However, I did talk to his mother, Eva. She says Charlie told her that he spoke with Janet Konow on the day he made the repairs and that he told her all about his problems with his wife, Desiree. It seems they're bad, but Eva won't say why. I think she's trying to protect her son, or maybe it's about Charlie's twin sister. She's due to deliver in three months and she knows nothing. I think Charlie and his mom wanted it that way."

"Thank you, Jordan." Johnathon turned his attention to advocate Alicia Townsend. "Status and by the way, why isn't Dr. Moss here?"

Cupping her hands on the table Alicia answered, "Dr. Moss asked me to come and speak for her because right now she and her staff are dealing with a lot of injured people. Eight men have lacerations and broken bones from trying to get at those two children, and the medical team is busy patching them up. As for Charlie, you've already heard. He was heavily medicated and strapped to a gurney. However, of immediate concern for Dr. Moss is Charlie's twin sister Judy. It appears that Desiree exploded emotionally in front of her. Between the stress of learning about Charlie's marital problems and that he is responsible for the death of these two children, it was more than she could handle. Simply put, she started bleeding, and Dr. Moss is fighting to save mother and baby."

Johnathon's head sunk into his hands. "Oh Lord, we've lost two beautiful children, and now we're at risk of losing a third and Charlie Cantrell could commit suicide. This is a terrible situation." He ran his finger through his thinning crop of gray-peppered hair. "Okay, let's go to open discussion. We know the bad news; we need to contain the situation so that it doesn't get worse. Your thoughts please."

Patrica was the first to speak up. From a security standpoint, Desiree Cantrell has become a loose cannon with her accusations and emotional outbursts. She's stirring the pot, and I suggest we lock her up in isolation to contain this needless incitement."

Johnathon called for the first vote of the meeting. "All in favor of ordering Desiree into lockup raise your hands to signify aye." All five hands shot up. "Patrica, get it done, now."

The security chief dutifully nodded in agreement and rising from her chair, she stepped back a few feet from the table. Taking hold of the PTT speaker microphone clipped to her shoulder and speaking in hushed tones, she instructed her Sergeant, and then took her place back at the table. "A security team is on the way, and Desiree will be in lockup within the next 10 minutes."

Johnathon nodded appreciatively and again fixed his attention towards Alicia. "Dr. Moss asked me to tell you that she's presently medicating Janet Konow with Fluoxetine."

"What's Fluoxetine?" Fante asked.

"Prozac."

"I thought we were all out of that stuff?"

"I know Fante, so did I. However, Dr. Moss seems to have a secret stash she keeps hidden away for days like this."

A faint smile crossed Jordan's lips, "Ahh, now, I know why you advocates call her the squirrel." It was a much needed humorous moment for everyone in the room.

Johnathon allowed a brief moment of relief and then refocused everyone's attention to the matters at hand. "Right now, there are two questions in my mind. First, can we save drift three? The second is what was happening between Charlie and Desiree Cantrell that was so disturbing that Charlie and his mother Eva would not tell Judy about it? My instincts tell me that there's something here that I need to dig into. So first off, what about three, Jordan, can we save it?"

"Aye, but the men are exhausted from retrieving the bodies of Janet's two children, God bless their souls. As for three, the cave-in made a mess of everything. Nobody is at risk now, but I don't want any more men injured because they are exhausted. Give me a few days to let them rest and to clean up the mess. Then I can make a detailed assessment."

"Yes, no more injuries." Johnathon agreed. "As it is, we've lost so much productivity with this situation. We'll no doubt need to dip into our emergency food supplies before this over, and I hate doing that." Johnathon then turned his attention to Fante.

"Fante, your group does the induction interviews, and you keep detailed records. Charlie Cantrell was a founding member and never went through an induction interview, but his wife Desiree did a year ago. Do you still have her induction interview results?"

"Yes! And they are detailed."

"Good. I want you to assemble everyone that was involved with her induction interview, and I want you to produce a detailed report and when I say detailed, I mean to leave no stone unturned. Can you put that report in my hands by this time tomorrow?"

"You'll have it by 9 AM tomorrow, Johnathon. I will personally see to it."

Johnathon's final question was for his advocate, Alicia Townsend. "Alicia, after I get Fante's report, I want to personally interview Janet Konow tomorrow afternoon. The last time I saw Janet was a few hours ago. She was in bad shape and who could blame her? First, her husband dies defending the community, and now she's lost her children. Still, we must get to the bottom of all this because I agree with Patrica, we need to get a handle on this before things get ugly. Do you think Janet Konow will be sufficiently stable tomorrow afternoon for me to have a useful conversation with her?"

"I see no reason why not, but I will immediately get with Dr. Moss and confirm this and let you know this afternoon."

"All right people, we plan the work; now let's work the plan. We will reconvene here in Chambers tomorrow evening after I have interviewed Janet Konow. Let's go to work."

Day 5 – Morning

In her youth, Fante Adebo's family had emigrated from Ghana to the US, and after a successful modeling career, she settled down to a happy life with a young Baptist minister. Proud of her heritage, she kept a good figure and even through the worst of the tribulation always managed to carry herself in a dignified way. But today, the middle-aged woman Johnathon saw, as she handed him her report, was deeply disturbed and exhausted with slumped shoulders. It was obvious that she and her team had been up all night because the folder was nearly 3/4 of an inch thick.

Johnathon pulled up a chair and patted the seat. "Sit beside me Fante." She complied without as much as a whisper.

"Why are you so sad Fante? Is it because of what you found in your induction interview records?"

She shook her head no. "We didn't find anything useful in the records, and I must have grilled my interviewers for hours."

"And why the sad face?"

"It's because of what we didn't discover."

"Continue."

"We were drawing a blank; so, I interviewed Eva, Charlie Cantrell's mother, early this morning. What I learned from her is that three months after Charlie and Desiree married, that Desiree told her husband that she had been sexually abused by three boys and that her father had done nothing about it. Eva also told me that Desiree had lied about that during her induction interviews."

"All of it?"

"Not all of it. When I checked the records, Desiree did admit that she had led a lascivious lifestyle as a young woman with many casual one nighters. However, she was asked three times by three different interviewers if she had a history of sexual, physical, or emotional abuse, and on each occasion she said, "No." I think I have a good team of interviewers, but this woman was a liar, and she pulled the wool over all of their eyes. I interviewed Desiree this morning in lock up, and she continues to maintain that she was never sexually abused as a child. So, this puts us in an awkward situation."

"Agreed, but if what you say is true, Patrica Heally will see this as an actionable offense; that is assuming we can corroborate Eva's story. Given that Charlie is heavily sedated and under a suicide watch that puts him out of the story for a while. Nonetheless, we need to get resolution on this ASAP."

Fante nodded in agreement. "If you want a resolution sooner than later, you have only one option, Janet Konow. Eva said that Charlie told her that he was forthcoming with her and that she knows everything."

"Did she say anything else?"

"Nothing useful."

Johnathon scratched the back of his neck for a bit and finally said, "I had a gut instinct yesterday this is how it would play out. So I guess the ball is in my court now."

"Good luck with Konow."

"Thanks but do us both a favor Fante. Take the afternoon off and get some rest. You look rode hard and put up wet, and I need you to be crisp and frosty for the council meeting this evening."

Fante patted him on the knee. "Will do, by the way, Jordan already fixed me up with a jar of his famous Scottish white lightning as he calls it. After the meeting, I think we'll both need a good jolt."

"I think you're right because we both know what this is leading up to." Fante nodded sadly in agreement.

Day 5 – Evening

All five members of the community Council convened as ordered by Johnathon, with Dr. Moss once again represented by Advocate Alicia Townsend. Johnathon began the meeting by first addressing Alicia. "Given that Dr. Moss is not here this evening, it appears that we still have a crisis demanding her attention."

"Yes," Alicia quietly answered. "At this moment, Dr. Moss is doing everything she can to save Judy Cantrell's baby and refuses to leave her side."

"Our thoughts and prayers are with Judy, and may God bless Dr. Moss with the gift of healing." A hearty round of amen was heard around the table.

"My friends, this evening we have only one issue to decide based on my interview this afternoon with Janet Konow. Janet confirmed with me everything that Eva has said to Fante about Desiree Cantrell's history of sexual abuse, which she withheld from us during her induction interviews. I have reviewed her induction documents in Fante's report, and she did in fact, sign our code of conduct agreement."

With that, Johnathon gave the Council a detailed account of his interview with Janet Konow. In closing he made one last, telling observation. "When I asked Janet why she did not come forward with information about how Charlie was obviously affected by his marital problems, she answered my question with a question."

Pausing for a brief moment, he took a deep breath, then sighed and continued. "Her question was 'Why did we knowingly allow an untreated sexual abuse victim into the community?'"

"In other words," he sighed. "There is blood is on our hands too, and to be honest, that's exactly how it feels to me."

"This is a question of guilt, not theatrics," Security Chief Patrica Healy tersely interjected. "Is Desiree Cantrell to be charged with treason by omission or not? That is the question."

"Yes, that is precisely the question before us this evening," Johnathon responded, "and it is a heavy one, because according to our code of conduct, there is only one penalty for treason, execution."

"Excuse me folks, I'm just a simple structural engineer," Jordan quipped, "Are we going to hang this woman by the neck until she is dead on a gallows that I will have to construct mind you? If so, then I damn well do not want people thinking that we sent her to her maker because she was raped as a 13-year-old girl."

Unfazed by Jordan's emotional outburst, Patrica calmly answered, "Jordan, the fact that she was raped as a 13-year-old girl is a moot point. There is only one thing that is relevant and which we must decide this evening. Did she intentionally and fraudulently withhold vital information during her induction interview? Also, it's important to note that she signed our code of conduct with the full understanding that the penalty for any form of treason is death."

"Yah, there's that" Jordan shot back, "but as they say, there is always two sides to every story."

This time, it was Fante who took on Jordan's emotional defense. "That's right Jordan. There are two sides to every story. Usually, the side people want to hear and the side they don't. I interviewed Desiree this morning, and she denied giving fraudulent answers during her induction interview to me also. However, we have two witnesses who say otherwise; a guilt-ridden husband who is on suicide watch, two dead children, and possibly a third. We could discount Eva as a mother defending her son, but Janet is a straight shooter. Desiree had her chance to tell her side this morning, and she lied – again."

Patrica noted Jordan's retreat from the argument. "Point taken, we are not, therefore, charging a woman for being raped as a 13-year-old girl. Rather, we are charging a liar whose intentional fraud resulted in the debilitation of her husband." Turning her head towards Jordan, she smartly lifted her chin, "A man that you, Jordan, have often described as the best man on your team."

"Well folks, there you have it," Johnathon glumly observed. "Patrica has clearly framed the issue and the decision we need to make. Rather than prolonging this dispiriting debate, I'm calling for an early vote. If it is unanimous, then Desiree Cantrell will be executed for the crime of treason by omission. If not, then we will reconvene in the morning, hear all sides, and then take another vote. Alicia, since you are Dr. Moss' proxy, you will vote for her. So, all who agree with the finding of treason by omission which carries the sentence of death raise your hands."

Four hands went up at a slowly staggered pace, except Jordan Campbell's. All eyes turned to him. "So, what do we call this, vengeance?" he spat.

For the first time that evening, Alicia spoke up. "No Jordan, it's not vengeance. It's a reckoning. Each day this drags on is another day of unnecessary risks. Given the daily struggle this community faces, we can ill afford the risk. We need a reckoning to settle accounts; so, we can get this community refocused on the existential business of surviving this miserable tribulation."

Biting his lip, Jordan looked at the advocate for the longest moment. He coolly gazed into her eyes; Alicia returned his gaze with a calm determination. "Bloody hell," he finally muttered as he slowly raised his hand. "May God have mercy on us all."

Day 8 – Morning

The execution of Desiree Cantrell was a sobering affair for the community; all were in attendance except those under medical care. Johnathon read the sentence and explained the judgment of the Council. Desiree Cantrell was then given her opportunity to make a final statement which she did. It was bitter. Resentful of her husband, she continued to maintain that he was at fault for everything.

Then, Johnathon did something that came as a surprise to everyone especially the other members of the Council. Before giving the order to pull the lever that would drop the floor panel below Desiree's feet, he announced that the bylaws of the community granted to him, as the leader of the community, the right to grant amnesty and announced an offer to the whole community. All those who had given fraudulent answers during their induction interviews would have 72 hours to come forward and confess their frauds. Those who did would be granted complete amnesty.

He also told the community, that he was doing this at the behest of Judy Cantrell. After Dr. Moss saved her baby, Johnathon visited her early that same morning. Still under the doctor's care, Judy was stable and asked that he visit her. It was then that she presented her amnesty proposal to him and he agreed because he saw it was a compassionate way to bring closure to this tragic event.

After the 72 hours had passed, by the final tally, five women and three men had come forward and confessed their frauds and were granted full amnesty.

Day 12 – Evening

Resting in his own compartment, Johnathon was pleased the community had managed to pull itself together so it could begin moving forward once again. Jordan Campbell had finally presented his engineering report on drift three that morning. It was salvageable and could be made safe again. He was relieved by that; it would relieve the crowding problem caused by the cave-in.

Charlie Cantrell was still on suicide watch, but Dr. Moss was confident he would recover. Meanwhile, his advocates, led by Alicia Townsend, were doing an excellent job of working with the children who had been upset by the execution. All in all, this dark chapter was coming to a close though he knew there would be more for this is the way of the tribulation. You soldier on and do the best you can.

As he was reviewing all this in his mind, his 12-year-old daughter, Pauline, came to sit by his side.

"I've been thinking about all of this daddy. About this woman we hung."

He turned to face her. "I know; I did not want to say anything until you were ready to talk about it."

Pauline fidgeted a bit and then reluctantly asked, "Daddy, I'll be 13 next year. If I'm raped, will you execute me for that?"

Pauline's question slammed his mind with the ferocity of Thor's hammer. Before he could gather himself, tears began streaming down his cheeks as he struggled to compose himself. Pauline hugged him, "Oh daddy, I'm so sorry for asking such a stupid question. Please don't cry."

Johnathon could only hold her close as warm tears continued streaming down his cheeks. "I'm sorry Daddy," Pauline repeated several times.

Finally, he was able to compose himself. Drawing a handkerchief from his pocket, he blew his nose and wiped the tears from his cheeks. "My darling, there are no stupid questions just stupid answers and yours was a good question." He lovingly kissed her forehead, "Some would say this woman was executed so little girls like you would never face the same fate. They think you and everyone else in the community would understand that lies kill and cannot be tolerated. This is especially true when those lies cost us our most precious treasures, our children."

"But is that how you would answer the question, Daddy?"

"No darling. I would answer it in another way. Do you remember last month during movie night when we watched the film, Titanic?"

"Oh yes, that's the one with the pretty lady who flew like a bird on the front of the ship."

"Yes, that's the one."

A puzzled expression came to her face "I don't understand Daddy. What does a sinking ship have to do with what happened to Desiree?"

Johnathon smiled tenderly. "Sweetheart, the sinking of the Titanic was a catastrophe. Do you know what a catastrophe is?"

"Something really awful that happens?"

"Fair enough, but do you know why catastrophes happen?"

Again she was puzzled, "I kind of think so, but I'm not really sure."

"Let me explain it to you then," he answered with a loving smile. "Catastrophes are the result of an unbroken chain of failures that culminate with a catastrophic failure event. This is why the Titanic sank. However, if something had broken the Titanic's chain of failures, all of those people would not have died such terrible deaths that night. Unfortunately for them, their chain of failures remained unbroken for many reasons, and all of them led to the same conclusion, a catastrophe."

"So what has this got to do with Desiree?"

"When Desiree did not tell the during her induction interview, she set in motion a chain of failure. Because she did not tell us the truth, which in this case we call omissions; those of us responsible for seeing this community through the tribulation were denied vital information. Had she been entirely truthful, we would have had the information we needed to break that failure chain and Janet Konow's two beautiful children would not be lying cold in their graves right now."

Pauline's eyes lit up. "Now I get it, daddy. Truth breaks the chain of failure and not telling the truth creates catastrophes."

"Brilliant observation, I could not have said it better myself." He hugged her lovingly. "I am so proud of you."

"I'm proud of you too Daddy, but I have one last question. If Desiree had been honest about what happened to her when she was a girl, how would you have broken her chain of failure?"

Johnathon looked deeply into her eyes because this was now a question they both shared. "Sweetheart that is the one question that still haunts me. How could we have broken Desiree's chain of failures in time to save Janet's children?"

"Let's find the answer together Daddy," Pauline cheerfully said.

"Perhaps we shall."

13

Abuse and Redemption

In the previous scenario, you may have asked, "Why execute Desiree? Why not just expel her from the community and let her fend for herself?"

That is a logical question to ask at this time. Turn a tap and you have freshwater; flip a switch and there is light; turn a dial and you have a comfortable home and hot water to bath in. Turn a key or press a button and go wherever you wish. If you are in trouble, dial 9-1-1; if you have pain, visit your doctor for a prescription. All of these things you can do presently except for one; imagine a time, when all you have is those with whom, you share a common purpose – that of survival.

Ergo, the many ...ologies, and ...isms that define your life today like many of the institutions we organize our lives around will fall away during the tribulation. The brutal reality of life will be at that point an existential awareness of what works and what hurts. With this in mind, I will now answer the question "Why execute Desiree?"

The answer comes in two parts. The first is that banishment would be a cruel and unusual punishment for Desiree. The second is that her banishment from the community would likely result in a well-organized attack that would claim many innocent lives and cause greater suffering. Husbands and fathers would die watching their wives and sisters and mothers and children being raped, murdered, and in some cases eaten. This may sound shocking to those with modern day flip-a-switch sensibilities; so let's reason it out together.

During the tribulation, your survival community will be surrounded by predators, gangs, warlords, cannibals, and so forth. Over time these predators will begin to disappear. Either turning upon themselves for lack of soft targets or, noble warriors will hunt them down and destroy them to protect their communities.

But one thing is certain; they will know you have what they desire, and they will be vigilant for opportunities exploit your weaknesses. If you banish Desiree, how far down the road will she get before these stalking monsters take her prisoner?

Then will come the torture, and it will be brutal. How long will it take for Desiree to break, once they begin burning her flesh with a propane torch? Not long and she will tell them everything she knows about your defenses, where your food stores are, how many men women and children are in the community, and above all your defense weaknesses. Once these monsters are confident they have all of the information they seek, they will do with Desiree as they please such as raping her to death. Is this not a cruel and unusual punishment? Is this too extreme?

No more extreme than the reality of a world where the collapse of governments and law and order gives way to anarchy. No more convenient water taps to turn, switches to flip, dials to twist, keys to turn, and help just three dialing digits away. Now ask yourself, are your present day sensibilities so precious that you need to blind yourself to this future reality?

Or more to the point, what happens when people are burying their loved ones because of your sensibilities? Will they see the spilling of their blood as necessary sacrifices to prop up your self-image?

Or will they view you as an existential threat and treat you accordingly? Before you shoot from the hip on this issue, I suggest you make a nice hot cup of tea, sit down in a quiet place, and project your mind into this bleak passage of time between this civilization and the next. Then make your call.

If you have been in awareness for years or perhaps since childhood, you've already been there and done that. If so, you are having the makings of a survival wellness advocate with a practical worldview, and you will accept the tragedy of Desiree as a fact of survival. Likewise, you will rise above flip-a-switch sensibilities to see how her treason left in its wake a diminished community and a tragic loss of life.

Conversely, as a sensitive person, you also see people holistically, and you know that executing people who lie about the abuses of their childhoods will only create further wounds. Therefore, as a teacher, mentor, and comforter, it is your responsibility to balance the security needs of the community with the emotional and mental needs of its members with histories of abuse.

This brings us to the one question that matters most and which was voiced by the character, Jonathon Brown. "How could we have broken Desiree's chain of failures in time to save Janet's children?"

With this in mind let's briefly re-examine the scenario. Desiree was the victim of sexual abuse. As a young girl of approximately 13 years of age, she was gang raped by three neighborhood boys. When she reported it to her father, he did nothing and abandoned her.

All of this dragged through her life like an emotional meat hook, and it took from her something very precious. All the joy of life she had as a 13-year-old girl was stolen from her that day and in a most vulgar way. Two wrongs do not make a right. So to say that such unfortunate souls must be excluded from survival communities is shortsighted and foolish.

According to a report published in 2010 by the U.S. Department of Health and Human Services, children are most vulnerable to child sexual abuse (CSA) between the ages of 7 and 13, and these horrible crimes are far more widespread than many would care to believe. 1 in 5 girls and 1 in 20 boys are CSA victims, and independent studies show even higher rates of abuse. Even worse, in 60% percent of the cases the perpetrator is typically a respected male within the child's social circle.

What this means for you as a survival wellness advocate is the leadership of your community should expect that one in five families will have a history of sexual abuse. While progress can be made with early treatment, untreated abuse such as shown in the example of Desiree only compounds the problem for everyone.

This will become even more prevalent during the tribulation, because there are different forms of abuse: sexual, emotional, and physical. Each can create emotional time bombs that will explode at the least opportune moments. Victims will either withdraw and become incapable of performing a vital role in the community, or as we see in the case of Desiree, they began acting out uncontrollably suppressed rage thereby perpetuating the cycle of victimization.

There will also be other issues to deal with as well sadly to say, but the elephant in the room will always be childhood sexual abuse. It, more than all other causes of disruptive and destructive behavior, will degrade the ability of survival communities to function, and will expose them to extreme harm and loss of life.

This issue goes to the existential survivability of the community because continuity of progeny is essential to its long-term viability. Throughout the history of humankind prior to World War II, our species had a reliable continuity of progeny. In other words there was a steady supply of populace in each age group along with a sufficient number of births to offset high mortality rates. It was a time of heartbreak and hardship; it will return again.

Does this justify male-dominated societies that treat women like baby breeders and children like unpaid farmhands? Of course not. This is not a noble model for survival when 90% of humanity will perish in the coming tribulation.

More to the point, for a man to subjugate a woman or child, he must first subjugate himself to a greater evil. Such men become abusive monsters and unworthy of God's love.

Therefore, for a survival community to remain viable, it must ensure its continuity of progeny which means that women and children need to be protected and cherished by the men of that community.

As a survival wellness advocate, you must employ a balanced effort.

On the one hand your highest calling is to be in service to the most vulnerable in the community, who will be women, children, the aged and infirmed.

On the other, the leadership of your community must encourage its men to support one another in the pursuit of their noble virtues. That a man's worth to the community is not measured with weapons, conquests, and loot. But rather, that their worth is measured in the admiring eyes of their families and community. Good men, one and all.

This brings us to Charlie. In the scenario, he was punished by Desiree for crimes he never committed. In our society of victimization, this has become acceptable with a twisted two wrongs make a right logic. Consequently, good men are led to the altar like naive lambs without knowing their wife's history, only to find themselves drawn into a cycle of abuse.

Statistically, less than 2% of men who marry under such circumstances know what they're getting into on their wedding day, and for the obvious reason.

The women know that if they divulge that information during the courtship, the likely result will be a termination of the engagement if not the relationship. So hoping against hope, they go to the altar thinking they can beat the odds, but they never do because two wrongs can never make a right.

It typically takes about three months after the marriage for the wife to become comfortable enough and drop her guard. That is when the hell is unleashed for these unwitting husbands and the mothers who raised them. The marriage then becomes a quagmire of grief.

To visualize this, imagine a marble tabletop polished to a glass-like finish. On the table are a large number of spinning tops, and all are turning in perfect unison and in a way that is magical. All is in balance and pleasing to the eye. But then, one top begins to wobble and then dips into a violent spin that sends it skittering across the table top and smashing into the other tops. In short order, the magical balance of the tabletop descends into chaotic ricochets.

Let's cut to the chase. What will be the impact of these human tragedies on the viability of a survival community, and who is at fault here?

The woman who was abused as a child and does not tell her husband until after their wedding day the sad story of her life? No.

The man who is incapable of finding enough love to rise above his disappointment and to shoulder the abuse of transference? No.

Then, if neither is at fault, who is?

For those who take a purely scientific view of this issue, it weaves itself into a series of rabbit holes and inconclusive results.

However, as a spiritual and sensitive person with a holistic view, finding fault is about understanding why sexual abuse lays the foundation for what I call energy parasitic events (EPE).

In order to understand this, we need to understand that when a child issexually abused, there will always be more than one perpetrator and they will come to take what they want, from various planes of existence.

Abuse and Triggers

In Surviving the Planet X Tribulation: A Faith-Based Leadership Guide, I explain in great detail about how the dark side uses our weaknesses to create conditions of fear and anger which in turn, cause us to release the life force energy they need to feed upon. In that book, I'm talking about egocentric people and such who are susceptible to this manipulation and who will refuse to believe they are being manipulated by the dark side.

However, in that book, I only address the threats we can see coming at us, such as character flaws that are easily observed. But as we see in this scenario, Desiree withheld her abuse history during her induction interviews essentially for the same reason that she withheld that information from her fiancé. Fear of rejection is the human side of this equation. Now let's discuss the other side.

Always remember that evil follows evil, and intention is the invitation.

In the case of child sexual abuse, the perpetrator typically stalks a child with the intention of abuse. This malevolent intention broadcasts a clear signal to the dark side that a feeding opportunity is at hand. Then when the abuse occurs, the child is violated on multiple levels.

There is the physical and emotional level of the perpetrator, during which the victim through fear-based emotion releases vast quantities of life force energy.

On another level, dark spirits operating on another plane of existence feed on this life force energy, while at the same time bonding triggers to the victim's memories of the abuse as it occurs.

Because of the violence of the crime, these memories are natural in origin and therefore indelible and completely lifelike. However, the triggers are unnatural implants affixed to these terrible memories by dark spirits during the crime.

Therefore the question is what purpose do these triggers serve? Their purpose is to create future energy parasitic events, which enable dark spirits to feed on the victims time and again, as well as all those within the victim's social network. Does this mean that an abused child is continually surveilled for feeding opportunities? No, because the trigger also acts as a sensor.

Think of it this way. How do we protect our homes? Very few can afford full-time security staffs, so the rest of us contract with alarm companies. These companies come to our house and office to install sensors in various areas. When a sensor is triggered, the company automatically places a 9-1-1 call for us.

In the case of the unnatural triggers implant by dark spirits alongside natural memories, these triggers will be sensitive to specific fear-based events. These events can seem trivial to some, like use of the word "sex" with the character, Desiree. Odd that something this innocuous can trip the alarm so to speak, yet this is how it works.

Once tripped, the trigger releases an invitation to the dark side for an EPE. Like prowling sharks that can smell traces of a victim's blood in the far distance, the dark spirits come to feed with a hunger for life force energy that is insatiable.

The dark spirits will do one of two things at this point; they'll release the trigger like opening a floodgate to slam painful memories of the abuse into victim's conscious mind, or they'll bide their time for an even larger meal. Do not forget; the dark side is methodical, paced, and persistent (MPP), and when they see an opportunity to expand the number of people they can feed on they take it. This is when timing becomes critical.

For example, Desiree may have set off the alarm on one day, but the dark spirits were patient and waited for a more opportune moment such as a holiday, anniversary or birthday. These are the days when people are more vulnerable because they expect to have a positive and loving experience.

When the trigger is released, like a floodgate, the memories of the abuse, regardless of when it happened, pour into the victim's conscious mind with all the force and horror of the initial event.

Then, like that top in our metaphor that starts to skitter across the tabletop, chaos ensues as everyone within range of the victim becomes involved. Their patience rewarded, the dark spirits sup upon a cornucopia of life force energy.

The horrible shame of abuse is that perpetrators set their victims up to become life force energy sows. In turn, dark spirits can milk them without compassion for the remainder of their natural lives.

This feeding is the insidious nature of the triggers implanted into sexual abuse victims by dark spirits during the commission of the crimes. It is also no wonder that counseling and pharmacological solutions tend to be more like emotional Band-Aids than permanent solutions.

Even worse yet, during the tribulation, there is going to be little time for such present-day treatments. So, what can be done to help these dear people who have been harmed so horribly?

When I began researching Planet X, I would have scoffed at what I am about to share with you. However, I have been doing this since 2002, and the work is transformative.

Science alone will always fall short of the measure, but when science is combined with the healing power of God's love, something magical happens. I call it the three stages of redemption.

Three Stages of Redemption

The first stage of redemption begins with the abuse victims. They must have the courage to take responsibility for their weaknesses which allowed the dark spirits to implant triggers within their memories. They cease being victims at that point, and instead become targets.

If that sounds odd, let's use an analogy that frames this in another way. What is the difference between being poor and broke? Here is the answer:

Seeing yourself as a poor person is a state of mind that will forever define your life. On the other hand, if you see yourself as being broke, that's a temporary financial condition which can be remedied.

So, when you identify yourself as a victim, you are adopting a state of mind that will define your life. As a target, however, you face a temporary condition that you can be remedied. That is if you are resolved to rid yourself of the triggers. How is this done?

Remember, memories of the abuse are natural and therefore indelible. Conversely though, the triggers implanted along with those memories are unnatural and here is where the healing power of God's love can become a game changer, but only when the target asks for it through prayer and a sense of personal responsibility.

Responsibility is the key word here because a victim bears no responsibility, whereas a target does. Therefore, because a victim bears no responsibility he or she feels entitled to act out their rage on innocent people. However, a target who does bear personal responsibility understands that they must not perpetuate the cycle of abuse by involving others that are innocent.

First Stage of Redemption

The manner in which a target shoulders this personal responsibility and takes the first step to healing begins with prayer. In essence the target resolves to give the triggers to God through divine intercession.

For example, "God, forgive me my weakness that has allowed dark spirits to implant within me these fearful triggers. I want to be free of their destructive aims; I want to be in service to those I love." Whether the triggers are removed with the first prayer, or with the one thousandth prayer makes no difference. The target must continue until he or she knows the triggers are gone. Testing it is easy. Use a trigger word, and see what happens.

Science cannot remove these triggers, and neither will the dark spirits that implanted them, but because they are unnatural in origin, God can expunge these triggers.

Once the target has given the triggers to God, they become beyond the meddling reach of the dark spirits, and the next stage of redemption becomes possible.

Second Stage of Redemption

Where the first stage of redemption is about removing triggers, the second stage is about sealing those wounds shut with what I call transference of ownership. Here is where you as a survival wellness advocate begin to play a critical role, based on discretion and compassion.

Those who see themselves as the victims of abuse will perpetuate a cycle of punishment upon themselves and those around them. Therefore the second step of redemption is about transferring ownership of the abuse.

This is done through forgiveness. This is a difficult concept for many to embrace, especially when painful memories torture them.

Much has been written about forgiveness and the whole topic can be rather complex and overwhelming. Therefore for the sake of expediency I offer a simple and workable definition of forgiveness that you may employ as an advocate.

Forgiveness is the cessation of judgment.

That's it. There is nothing more.

Forgiveness is the cessation of judgment.

When the target ceases to judge the perpetrator for the abuse, something wonderful can happen. Ownership of the abuse can then revert to the perpetrator hen targets say, "This was of your making and now you own it all to yourself."

When you are asked about vengeance, stress that transference of ownership by forgiveness or by other means is preferable to vengeance. This is because even when victims avenge themselves upon the abuser, ownership of the abuse can remain with the victim. It is why vengeance is often a hollow victory.

What if the abuser is alive and a part of the target's life? This is a very important question due to the fact that entire families will be inducted into survival communities. Abusive family members are also not likely to change their behavior. Instead, the stresses of survival will more than likely exacerbate their abusive tendencies.

Therefore, as a survival wellness advocate, your discretion must be beyond question, especially regarding the most vulnerable in the community. All must trust your discretion on a level comparable to that of a physician, lawyer or a priest. Otherwise, any indiscretions on your part will only serve to aide and abet ongoing abuse situations, and you eventually will be shunned by the community.

With that, we come to the other essential aspect of your role, your compassion. Here is where you must engage the community as a whole to help targets with a realistic, goal-driven process as part of the third stage of redemption.

Third Stage of Redemption

While we can use pharmaceuticals, alcohol, and illegal drugs to mask and suppress our memories, they are always there, just beneath the fog of stupor. Such is the case for the target once God has taken the triggers away and the ownership of the abuse has been transferred to the perpetrator.

Therefore the third stage of redemption is that the target and the community accept that the memories of the abuse are an indelible dark stain and that they must be dealt with.

Through the healing power of God's love and the support of the community, the target can find a purpose in life to lighten the stains of terrible memories. While these memories can never completely fade away, the goal is to bleach them to a point where they are tolerable enough for the target to pursue some semblance of a normal life. Ideally, this will happen with a combination of spiritual and scientific support.

The target must not only pray for God's help in finding a worthy purpose, but they must also be forthcoming and honestly approach those in the community with the knowledge, experience, and desire to help them achieve the promise of a workable life.

Here is where psychologists and counselors are wonderful resources as problem solvers. Use them in any other way, and they become emotional Band-Aid dispensers. Likewise, spiritual leaders with abuse counseling experience are wonderful solution resources as well.

Another important consideration is community consensus.

Everyone in the community, especially psychologists, and counselors must present a unified front. Once a trusted person says to a target, "I believe this but not that," the target will become confused and doubtful. This doubt can the can cause the entire process of redemption to collapse.

Again, everyone who works with the target must be on the same page.

But what about the everyday people in the target's life? They too must be on the same page and earnest about being committed to the target's success. Here is where you as the survival wellness advocate can help them to organize their support efforts effectively.

Likewise, it is imperative they positively affirm the target's individual responsibility through all three stages, without rewarding disruptive behaviors with pity or sympathy. In other words, tough love.

For the community, the obvious need is to break the chain of failures and the benefit is equally obvious. With love, compassion, and understanding targets will have a clear path to a life as a fully functional, loyal, productive and valued member of the community.

However, there is a second transcendent benefit. It will do more than reward the community for its love, support, and compassion. It will reach far beyond the community, through righteous voices of change.

Righteous Voices for Change

The one thing I have not shared with you up to this point and which I will now close with is the transformative effect of making a commitment of Perpetual Genesis in service to God's mission, through service to others.

For those who have made more personal commitments, the question they will repeatedly ask during the tribulation, shall be, "what is the meaning of all this?"

As a Perpetual, the question you will often ask is, "what is the meaning of what I have learned?" This is the crux of this transformative process and the centeredness you will acquire using this process. I can tell you, that it is often a difficult and daunting journey, but one that tends to reach hopeful destinations.

So why do I say this? I want to share with you the hopeful destination I've found in the course of writing this book.

Did I Miss Something?

Writing a book is like making a baby elephant with lots of trumpeting and heavy pounding. But with patience and persistence something of size will eventually fall out of the process. After that, questions begin to form in your mind, and for me, those questions typically go to completeness. Was the book faithful to its the original thesis, did I miss something or was there something I could have done better?

After I sent my book *Being In It for the Species: The Universe Speaks* to Press in 2014, that last question haunted me. What could I have done better?

This book was a first of a kind for me because it was primarily comprised of channeled readings with multiple Guides conducted with the help of an internationally celebrated psychic. When you receive knowledge in this unique way, you begin to see patterns form over time as issues of great importance to the message givers.

With this book, two notable drumbeat issues emerged. This is because these issues recur in the readings time and again. The most prevalent issue was the use of the word "unshackled." The Guides presently see us as a species shackled by slavers, but as a result of the flyby of the Planet X System and resulting tribulation, we will become temporally unshackled as a species.

Though we will die in vast numbers, we will nonetheless die as free men, women, and children and those on the other side of the veil cared deeply about this.

The Guides want to help as many to survive as possible, and of equal importance to them is that we emerge from this tribulation as a permanently unshackled species. It is why they take great pains to explain what the elitists, whom they view as slavers, will do to trick humanity into allowing itself to be reshackled into slavery, and what we can do to prevent that.

The second most prevalent drumbeat message from the Guides was about the women who would be abducted with the help of our governments and institutions by the Annunaki. This is an alien race intertwined with the history of our species, and who, according to the ancient Sumerian texts, are responsible for the creation of modern man. This was not for a noble cause but to serve as a genetically engineered hybrid slave species.

At the outset of the Tribulation, the Annunaki will return, and this will forever alter how we see ourselves as a species.

The concerns expressed by the Guides for these abducted women are profound, and the mention of them recurs time and again throughout the book. Rather than describing what was in these readings, I have assembled a collection of snippets from *Being In It for the Species: The Universe Speaks,* and I have rearranged them into the following summary:

"Like grave robbers stealing in the night, the Annunaki will come for gold and the flesh of women ordained by their progeny as gifts of conquest for the procreation of slaves destined for another world.

When the Annunaki take your women for breeding purposes, to create slaves elsewhere in the solar system, the reality of this will strike human consciousness like the hammer of a brass bell.

Virgins of noble character and temperament are swept away from home and kin without ceremony, nor sympathy. Their lives being deemed fit for the betterment of an elite few; they will be gently herded into the great ships of the Annunaki. Their fate will be to breed a new race of slaves to replace those destroyed in a rebellion on another world.

Their treatment will be fair and their conditions comfortable, so they will breed emotionally healthy children for indoctrination by others, who once they've been weaned, will become the only parents these hybrid children will ever have known. Memories of their birth mothers will be denied them, and the memories of creation and enslavement will be wiped from the minds of most of these women. For a few, stubborn memories will endure, like for those abducted throughout the centuries by races who view life on this world as sub-ordinate to their own.

These women will come home, lost like sheep without their shepherds. Their memories stripped bare they will be secreted away, yet in time, stories of what was done to them will become known to all. From amongst these women will come a courageous few whose memories endure in fragments of sorrow.

These women will preach to the world the price of freedom and the shame that comes from one species allowing itself to be used to shackle another, worse yet to give life into shackles without even the smallest taste of freedom."

As the author of the book, it was my responsibility to convey these messages from the Guides to the reader. While I believe I satisfied that obligation, I nonetheless remained haunted by a troubling question. What could I have done better for these noble and unfortunate women? Or more specifically, what could I have shared in that book that would've been useful in helping them to deal with what can only be imagined as an inhuman and alien form of sexual abuse.

Here is where I felt that I had somehow failed these women; I also knew that this could not stand. Somehow or in some way, I needed to find a way to help these precious women to heal from the shameful things done to them, and for them to become the righteous voices of change. They shall "preach to the world" as the Guides put it, with a noble message for the freedom of our species.

The Search for Answers

I said this before; this work is transformative. Because, when you commit yourself to God's mission of Perpetual Genesis, you begin seeking questions to the answers that reach beyond the body of humankind's knowledge of the world. This creates a classic chicken or the egg dilemma.

Did you incarnate to seek these answers and thereby set yourself into circumstances which create the questions, or is it less ordered than that? Is it because we incarnate to learn how to responsibly exercise free will, and these thorny questions are the twists and turns of an unpredictable process?

The only thing I know for certain is regardless of how these questions come into being patience is necessary for the answers. In a manner of speaking, you stuff your questions into glass canning jars, seal them shut, and then set them on a shelf. After that, you wait for the universe to fax you the answer so you can paste a label on the jar.

As to the chicken or the egg dilemma, I'm still waiting for the fax to arrive.

However, for the question about how I could help these unfortunate noble women, that jar is now labeled, and it reads "Abuse and Redemption." Now, the only thing left to decide is an appropriate time for us to take the jar down from the shelf and to open it, and there is an answer to that too.

Freedom

The Guides tell us, "Virgins of noble character and temperament are swept away from home and kin without ceremony, nor sympathy." They also tell us they are returned. This is when we must all shower them with love and support, for the remainder of their natural lives.

When they return, there will be a handful of noble and compassionate nations that take them in. Amongst them will be those whose lives are forever shattered; there will likewise be those who will find their purpose in life as righteous voices of change.

Eventually, the Annunaki return these unfortunate women, and this is when the elites will see the mood of the world change.

That is when they will go into spin mode. They will posit arguments in support of their duplicity and these arguments will be like painted rust, bright and cheerful on the outside, but beneath that something ugly. Old and brittle it will harken to sad moments when women and girls were sacrificed by barbaric cultures to appease imaginary and angry deities. The elites will nonetheless hail these women with parades and speeches and prolifically thank them for their service to humanity before sweeping them under the carpet.

But these women will not go quietly into the night for this is not God's intention for them. They shall become a sisterhood of freedom and the most righteous voices of change our planet has ever known. When that time comes, we must celebrate them, listen to them, shield, and protect them.

Until then, we know that they will be taken, used, and returned like abused indentured servants. Likewise, we now know how to help them once they have been returned.

Therefore there is one last question.

What can we do to help them before they are taken off the world for this hideous and alien sexual abuse of motherhood? We must give them something to hold onto. It must be simple and said time and again.

In closing, I ask you, dear reader, to contemplate this and to draft a simple message of hope that these women can take with them as they are taken from our world. And if I am so fortunate as to be alive at that time, I know what my simple message to them will be.

"You are Earth Mothers and your return is your right. We embrace you as mothers would embrace their daughters with understanding and unconditional love. We await your return to us."

Marshall Masters
Chief Steward
Knowledge Mountain
Church of Perpetual Genesis

Alphabetical Index

68869174R00097

Made in the USA
Middletown, DE
02 April 2018